The Age GRACEfully Cookbook

The Power of FOODTRIENTS to Promote Health and Well-being for a Joyful and Sustainable Life

Grace O

creator of FOODTRIENTS

Skyhorse Publishing

Skyhorse Publishing books may be purchased in bulk at special discounts for sales promotion, corporate gifts, fund-raising, or educational purposes. Special editions can also be created to specifications. For details, contact the Special Sales Department, Skyhorse Publishing, 307 West 36th Street, 11th Floor, New York, NY 10018 or info@skyhorsepublishing.com.

Skyhorse® and Skyhorse Publishing® are registered trademarks of Skyhorse Publishing, Inc.®, a Delaware corporation.

Visit our website at www.skyhorsepublishing.com.

10 9 8 7 6 5 4 3 2 1

Library of Congress Cataloging-in-Publication Data is available on file.

Cover design: David Ter-Avanesyan and Brian Peterson
Cover photo credit: Matthew Fried
Designer: Lynn Fleschutz
Photographer: Matthew Fried
Nutrition Consultant: Monica Reinagel, MS, LN, CNS

The recipes and information in this book do not replace advice from a doctor or qualified health practitioner. Always consult your health practitioner before changing any routine in your lifestyle, including diet and exercise. The author and publisher disclaim all responsibility for any loss or liability incurred as a result of using this book.

Hardcover ISBN: 978-1-63450-378-5
Paperback ISBN: 978-1-5107-6899-4
Ebook ISBN: 978-1-63450-384-6

Printed in China

Contents

Contents

Acknowledgments

I have written this cookbook to honor and thank my loving parents. My mother taught me how to cook and her lessons have inspired many of the recipes I am sharing with you on these pages. My work is also influenced by my father, a doctor who imparted to me his knowledge about how our bodies change over a lifetime. My mother's original recipes have been adapted to incorporate what I have since learned about healthy cooking and anti-aging foods. I also thank my sweet husband, Rupert, who never complained about the endless parade of staff who helped me perfect each recipe over the last two years.

Heartfelt thanks go to my dedicated food preparation, styling, and test kitchen team, Angie Abrantes, Jean Paul Dellosa, Leandra Gepielago, Ma Carmen Juco, and Milagros Vilar, and to my researcher, Maria Inciong. Wonderful ideas from Diane Assad, Diana Marie Bruen, and Jarmila Kelly have enhanced many of my recipes. Thanks also go to photographer Matthew Fried, whose creativity and attention to detail resulted in mouth-watering images. Angela Pettera improved my recipes wonderfully by contributing both her writing skills to the text and her perceptive eye as photo stylist, adding a sense of home and warmth to Matthew's photographs.

Shelly Kale expertly edited the manuscript and managed the publication process. Lynn Fleschutz's and Barbara Weller's extraordinary sense of color and typography gave the book's design a unique appeal. Cynthia Cleveland, Nancy Cushing-Jones, and Barbara Weller, the partners of Broadthink, provided invaluable advice on all aspects of this project.

Finally, thanks must be given to my healthcare employees, especially Nancy O'Connor, who had a little less time with me these last two years while I pursued this personal venture. And a special acknowledgment goes to Vic Perez, whose belief in me and unending enthusiasm kept me going, no matter how hectic my schedule or how full my calendar.

Foreword

As an anti-aging practitioner, I have learned that if you want to look and feel young, it is essential to have an anti-aging strategy—regardless of age. Research has proven that just by making some adjustments to your lifestyle, you can prevent many of the physical and mental signs of aging—keeping you youthful long into your 90s!

When I talk to my patients about anti-aging techniques, they're often surprised to learn that aging is nothing more than a collection of symptoms telling you that your body isn't repairing and reproducing itself the way it should. You likely do not get enough sleep and exercise, and you have created serious deficits in vital nutrients.

One of the most important strategies I recommend to my patients is paying more attention to optimum nutrition. Believe it or not, there is such a thing as an anti-aging diet. It provides the type of nutrition that supports good levels of human growth hormone (HGH), the substance that keeps us young, and high-powered antioxidants, which keep cells strong and healthy.

When I advise my patients to be mindful of the foods they eat in order to keep themselves looking and feeling good, I'm often asked the same question: What are the best foods for me to cook with in order to stay healthy? A key answer to this question is eating meals with a variety of whole foods—foods that have undergone minimal processing and are classified as nutrient-rich. This means that they contain vitamins, minerals, phytonutrient antioxidants, fiber, protein, Omega-3 fatty acids, and anti-inflammatories—all the protective qualities nature has to offer. Indeed, the best diet is one that is based on whole foods with minimal processing, regardless of how many grams of carbohydrates, protein, or fat they contain.

Grace O's *The Age GRACEfully Cookbook: The Power of FOODTRIENTS to Promote Health and Well-being for a Joyful and Sustainable Life* is a new anti-aging cookbook that makes an important contribution to this discussion. By incorporating whole foods into her ingredients, she shows you how to maximize your intake of powerful nutrients at every meal. From foods known for their whole-food benefits, to spices that boost your immunity and reduce swelling, to super foods whose antioxidants, nutrients, and fiber increase your anti-aging capabilities, FoodTrient recipes help not only to fight aging from the inside, but also to smooth lines, wrinkles, and uneven skin tone on the outside.

Getting older is inevitable. However, aging doesn't have to be. Growing older gracefully is what you want to strive for—staying vital and active and able to participate in every aspect of your life with each passing year.

Mark A. Rosenberg, MD
The Institute for Healthy Aging

Introduction

We all want to be healthy and look and feel young. Today, scientists have identified many strategies for wellness that help prevent disease and slow the aging process, including what we eat and how we prepare our foods.

For example, antioxidants in fruits and vegetables can reduce the risk of cancer by fighting damage to our cells and chromosomes caused by free oxygen radicals. Polyunsaturated fats, such as Omega-3 fatty acids, can protect our hearts by lowering cholesterol and triglyceride levels in the blood. Certain foods, such as ginger and mustard, can keep our arteries healthy and our skin from swelling by reducing inflammation. Vitamin E can help us look our youngest by strengthening our hair and skin. But many of us don't know how to make sure that our diets give us the health benefits we want and need.

Growing up in a family of chefs and restaurateurs in the Philippines, I learned from an early age how to make healthy, savory meals with natural ingredients. I was encouraged to experiment in the kitchen and taught with my mother in her culinary arts school. Later, when I opened my own restaurants, the country's rich natural resources—endless sources of vegetables, fruits, and fish—provided opportunities both to innovate and adapt classic dishes. When I moved to the United States in 1989, I began work in the healthcare field, eventually owning and operating skilled nursing facilities. My work with aging populations has brought a new element to my passion for healthful cooking, and I've spent the last twenty years investigating natural ingredients that help me feel my best.

Combining what I've learned with the latest scientific research, I've created delicious recipes using super foods and ingredients with essential health and anti-aging benefits. These dishes feature a wealth of vitamins, minerals, antioxidants, anti-inflammatories, and a host of other beneficial compounds—what I call FoodTrients—not found in the highly processed foods that you pick up in the prepared foods section of the supermarket or at the drive-through. And they taste great!

The recipes in this book, many of them quick and easy to prepare, are simple ways to cook delicious meals with unique ingredients, such as ginger root, turmeric, and moringa, and more familiar fare, such as blueberries, cinnamon, and soy—everything you need to look and feel younger on the inside and on the outside. Welcome to a younger, healthier you!

Getting Started

Whether you're twenty-one or over fifty, your health is important. And what supports a healthy body more—inside and out—than the foods you eat? The recipes in this cookbook are designed to make good food loaded with anti-aging ingredients a joy to eat. Here's some basic information to help you maximize your enjoyment from your *The Age GRACEfully Cookbook*.

What Is a FoodTrient?

Wholesome foods have nutrients our bodies need to maintain optimum function. The recipes in this book are presented around an organizing principle I call FoodTrients— twenty-six powerful nutrients that promote health, wellness, and longevity.

FoodTrient Properties

I have determined five categories of FoodTrients that are essential to age-defying and healthful living. Specially designed logos represent each category and are included with every recipe, summarizing the healthful properties of the ingredients. By incorporating these properties into your everyday diet, you are more likely to look and feel younger, have more energy, and improve your mood and mind. Who knew that the right foods in sufficient amounts could do so much good for your body? Now we have the science to prove it.

 Anti-inflammatory Reduces inflammation process in cells, tissues, and blood vessels, helping to slow aging and reduce the risk of long-term disease

 Antioxidant Prevents and repairs oxidative damage to cells caused by free radicals

 Disease-Preventing Reduces risk factors for common degenerative and age-related diseases

 Immunity Booster Supports the body's resistance to infection and strengthens immune vigilance and response

 Mind and Beauty Encourages vibrant skin and hair and improves mood and mental agility

Getting started

Finding FoodTrients in the Recipes

Accompanying each recipe is a list of its FoodTrients. I explain how these key ingredients defy aging and its effects with the specific foods, herbs, and spices that help keep skin looking younger, prevent the diseases of aging, and increase energy and vitality. You can get the most benefit from FoodTrients when they become the mainstay of your everyday diet, not from any one recipe.

FoodTrients at a Glance

The chart on pages 146–153 identifies the FoodTrients in my recipes, their sources, and their benefits to your health and well-being.

Whole Foods

My recipes are made with whole foods. This means that I have used ingredients that are unprocessed and unrefined to maximize their nutritional benefits. Whenever possible, I buy organic, seasonal foods. I use fresh fruits, vegetables, and spices instead of canned, frozen, or dried varieties; grass-fed beef instead of grain-fed beef; free-range, hormone-free poultry instead of farmed; fresh fish instead of frozen; low-fat or nonfat dairy products; and butter and sugar substitutes. Combining preservative-free foods that contain age-defying attributes with delicious, easy-to-make recipes is a sure path to achieving a joyful, sustainable life!

These days, wholesome foods are more available than they were even a few years ago. You can find them at supermarkets, health food and ethnic food stores, food co-ops, farmers' markets, and online.

Ingredients

I am constantly creating recipes that are built on the foundations of modern scientific research and ancient knowledge of medicinal herbs and natural ingredients from cultures all around the world. With this book, you will learn the health benefits of many familiar and unfamiliar ingredients and how to incorporate them in easy-to-follow recipes. Some of the more unusual ingredients may be unfamiliar to you, but my family has used them in our cooking for generations. They are gaining recognition for their flavor and healthful properties.

Açaí Juice

The Açaí berry fruit is grown on the banks of the Amazon River in Brazil and Peru, but it's readily available in the United States as a juice, powder, fruit pulp, and even nutritional supplement.

Bitter Melon

This tropical vine produces one of the most bitter fruits you'll find, but I soak it in salted water to remove the bitterness. It's delicious! Bitter melon is often used in Chinese soups and teas, but it's popular throughout Southeast Asia.

Chia

Most Americans probably know about chia seeds only through Chia Pets—those clay animals that grow a luxurious coat of chia sprouts when watered. But chia is becoming known for more than just decoration. The flowering chia plant is a member of the mint family and is native to Guatemala and southern and central Mexico. I have read that the word *chia* comes from the Mayan language and means "strength."

Hemp Milk

This creamy dairy alternative is made from hemp seeds that are soaked and ground into water. It is used in vegan and vegetarian cooking. I like its taste, and its texture is smoother than another popular dairy alternative, soy milk.

Jackfruit

The tropical jackfruit tree is part of the mulberry family and is native to southern and Southeast Asia. It has been cultivated in India for thousands of years. Its fruit contains an edible pulp and nutritious seeds. Fresh jackfruit is hard to find and is harvested only from late spring to late summer, but you can buy canned ripe jackfruit year round.

Moringa

Moringa plants from Africa and Asia are now cultivated in the United States. Their leaves and the powders, teas, and flakes produced from them are used in cooking. Eaten fresh, the leaves give off a slightly grassy flavor. The moringa plant is harvested seasonally and is not available year round, but you can substitute moringa powder instead of the fresh leaves.

Soursop

This small tree of tropical South America comprises about 150 species and its fruit can weigh up to 8 pounds. The creamy pulp of the fruit is often used in ice cream and as a juice.

Turmeric

This member of the ginger family is native to tropical Southeast Asia. Its long, slender roots are commonly used as a spice in curries. I have found that its juice is a nice addition to a healthful diet.

Substitutes

Butter

I use a butter substitute when I make desserts to cut down on saturated fat. I prefer Smart Balance 50/50 Butter Blend for its taste and ease in cooking.

Getting started

Sugar

Many people depend on sugar substitutes to cut calories from their drinks and desserts and for other health reasons, but the majority are made from unnatural ingredients. There are many natural sugar substitutes on the market, but I use an all-natural product, Whey Low® Gold brown sugar substitute, which you can purchase online. This blend of simple sugars is derived from whey—the watery part of milk that separates from the curds in the process of making cheese. It tastes exactly like sugar, is perfect for baking, and you use less of it than other sugar substitutes to achieve the same results. In any recipe, you can use the same amount of Whey Gold as sugar. Other natural sweeteners I like to use are agave nectar, natural cane sugar, honey, date sugar, brown rice syrup, maple sugar, and blackstrap molasses.

Salt

Today, many people are putting aside ordinary table salt and using a variety of different salts to enhance the flavor of foods. I prefer sea salts and kosher salt for their pure, bright flavors. Sea salt is not as refined as table salt and contains traces of other beneficial minerals, while kosher salt is free of additives, lighter, and more easily dispersed than table salt. Salt substitutes are also available for people who are on low-salt diets.

Testing for Doneness

As a basic rule, food safety experts recommend using an instant-read thermometer—readily available at markets and cookware shops—to check the doneness of poultry and meat. For chicken, the thermometer should read 170° F for white meat and 180° F for dark meat. For beef, cook to 125° F for rare, 145° F for medium rare, 160° F for medium, and 180–195° F for well done. To test the doneness of fish, I usually wait until the fish breaks into clean flakes when pressed. Some cooks rely more on other, low-tech methods to test for doneness: for chicken juices to run clear or for the fish to look opaque, for example. Regardless, your goal is to find the right combination of taste and food safety.

Cookware

Certain acidic fruits—including cranberries, strawberries, and mango—require nonreactive cookware, such as copper or enamel-coated cast iron, to keep the acid they produce from interacting with the metal. If you have only aluminum cookware, here's a neat trick my mother taught me: drop a cleaned penny into the pot. The copper in the penny will keep the acid from reacting with the aluminum. Just remember to remove the penny before serving! I also use enamel-coated cast iron cookware when cooking meat and poultry for its tenderizing effect.

Starters

FOODTRIENTS

Isoflavones
Omega-3s
Selenium
Zinc

Soy Custard Cups

This dish is an interesting way to add more soy to your diet. The isoflavones in soy may help maintain bone density, reduce the risk of certain cancers, protect against heart disease, and alleviate symptoms of menopause. The Omega-3s in the tofu help skin retain its natural moisture. This recipe is inspired by the Chinese steamed custards served at dim sum. You can put almost anything under the silken tofu layer, and the garnishes are endless.

1. Drain the tofu and press between paper towels to remove excess water. Place in a blender or food processor with the salt and mix until texture is smooth, about 1 minute.

2. In a medium bowl, rehydrate the shiitake mushrooms in hot water for 20 minutes. Drain and chop.

3. Mince the shrimp. Heat the peanut oil in a sauté pan over medium-high heat and sauté the shrimp, mushrooms, and chives for 5–7 minutes. Season with the salt and pepper.

4. Divide the shrimp mixture among four small ramekins and top with tofu.

5. Cover ramekins with foil and place in a steamer pot. Cover pot and steam until the tofu is set, about 15–20 minutes.

6. Top with your choice of garnish and serve warm.

Serves 2–4

1 package (8 oz.) silken tofu

Pinch of salt

10–12 dried shiitake mushrooms

¼ lb. peeled shrimp (devein, if desired)

2 Tbs. peanut oil

2 Tbs. chopped chives

Sea salt and ground pepper to taste

Soy sauce, ponzu sauce, chopped scallions, slivered radishes, or black sesame seeds as garnish

FOODTRIENTS

Chlorophyll
Choline
Fiber
Lycopene
Sulfur compounds

Ai Ao DP MB

Quinoa Tabbouleh on Pita

Quinoa is a nutrient-dense ingredient that acts as a complete protein. It also has silica for building collagen, which helps keep your skin's elasticity. The tomatoes provide lycopene, the parsley gives us chlorophyll and antioxidants, and the olive oil helps lower inflammation.

1. Combine the quinoa and salted water in a saucepan and cook, covered, over medium-high heat for 20 minutes. Allow to cool.

2. Toss quinoa with the parsley, tomatoes, scallions, 3 Tbs. of the olive oil, lemon juice, salt, pepper, and sumac.

3. To make the pita rounds, preheat oven to 400 degrees. Brush pitas with the remaining 1 Tbs. olive oil. Cut pitas into triangles, wrap in foil, and toast in the oven at 400 degrees for 10 minutes.

Serves 2

½ **cup quinoa**

½ **tsp. kosher salt dissolved in 1 cup water**

2 cups finely chopped parsley

½ **cup diced plum tomatoes or halved grape tomatoes**

3 Tbs. chopped scallions

4 Tbs. olive oil

2 Tbs. lemon juice (about 1 lemon)

Sea salt and ground pepper to taste

Pinch of sumac

3 whole-wheat pita rounds

body
rejuvenator

FOODTRIENTS

Allicin   Selenium
Isoflavones   Zinc
Oleocanthal
Omega-3s

Garlic Crab Royale

Crab provides the selenium in this dish while garlic brings a host of impressive health benefits to the table through the compound allicin. Allicin has been shown to lower cholesterol, reduce plaque buildup in arteries, and keep blood platelets from sticking together too aggressively. I've served this dish to presidents and to royalty. It consistently wins raves.

1. Steam the crabs in a stockpot for 20 minutes. Smaller crabs may be done sooner. Remove crabs and set aside.

2. In a small saucepan, combine the soy sauce, sugar, mirin, lime juice, and pepper. Cook over low heat for 5 minutes. Set aside.

3. Heat the oil in a large wok or skillet over medium-high heat. Sauté the garlic cloves until brown, about 3–4 minutes. Set aside half the sautéed garlic.

4. Add the soy sauce mixture to the wok. Add the crabs, cut side down. Cover wok and cook for 5 minutes.

5. Remove cover and boil crabs for 8–10 minutes.

6. Add the scallions and cook for 2 minutes.

7. Turn crabs in wok until evenly coated with sauce. Remove and serve with reserved garlic.

Serves 2–4

2 large Dungeness crabs, cut in half, or 4 small whole crabs

½ cup soy sauce

¼ cup sugar

¼ cup mirin (seasoned rice wine)

¼ cup lime juice (about 2 limes)

Pinch of ground pepper

¼ cup olive oil

Cloves of 1 head of garlic

3 scallions, cut into long strips

FOODTRIENTS

Anthocyanins   Potassium
Carotenoids   Quercetin
Fiber   Sulfur compounds
Lycopene   Vitamin C
Oleocanthal

Moringa Vegetable Soup

In Africa and Asia, where moringa plants grow in abundance, people add the tiny leaves to soups and stews just before serving. The leaves are wilted by the hot liquid but are not fully cooked, so their vitamins stay intact. I also like the flavor of moringa combined with squash, eggplant, and okra (another African ingredient). For this soup, any smoked fish, such as salmon, can be used. To make this soup vegan, use vegetable stock in place of the chicken stock and omit the fish or fish sauce. To give this soup an Asian flair, add 1 tablespoon of gingerroot, cut into strips.

1. In a large saucepan or Dutch oven, boil the squash or pumpkin in the chicken stock for 10 minutes.

2. Add the eggplant, okra, and string beans, and boil the vegetables until they are tender, about 7–10 minutes.

3. While the soup is cooking, heat the oil in a sauté pan over medium-high heat. Add the garlic and onion and stir-fry until the onion is translucent, about 3 minutes.

4. Add the tomato to the sauté pan and continue cooking for 3 minutes. Add the flaked fish or fish sauce and cook an additional 5 minutes.

5. Remove soup from heat and stir in the sauté mixture. Add the moringa leaves or powder. Season with the salt and pepper.

Serves 2–4

2 cups diced kabocha squash or pumpkin, seeds removed and rind on

1 quart chicken stock

¾ cup diced eggplant

9 pieces okra, cut in halves or thirds

¾ cup cut string beans

¼ cup olive oil

2 tsp. minced garlic

½ cup diced onion

¾ cup diced medium tomato

¼ lb. flaked smoked fish or 1 Tbs. fish sauce

½ cup fresh moringa leaves or 1 Tbs. moringa powder dissolved in 3–4 Tbs. warm water

Sea salt and ground pepper to taste

skin strengthening

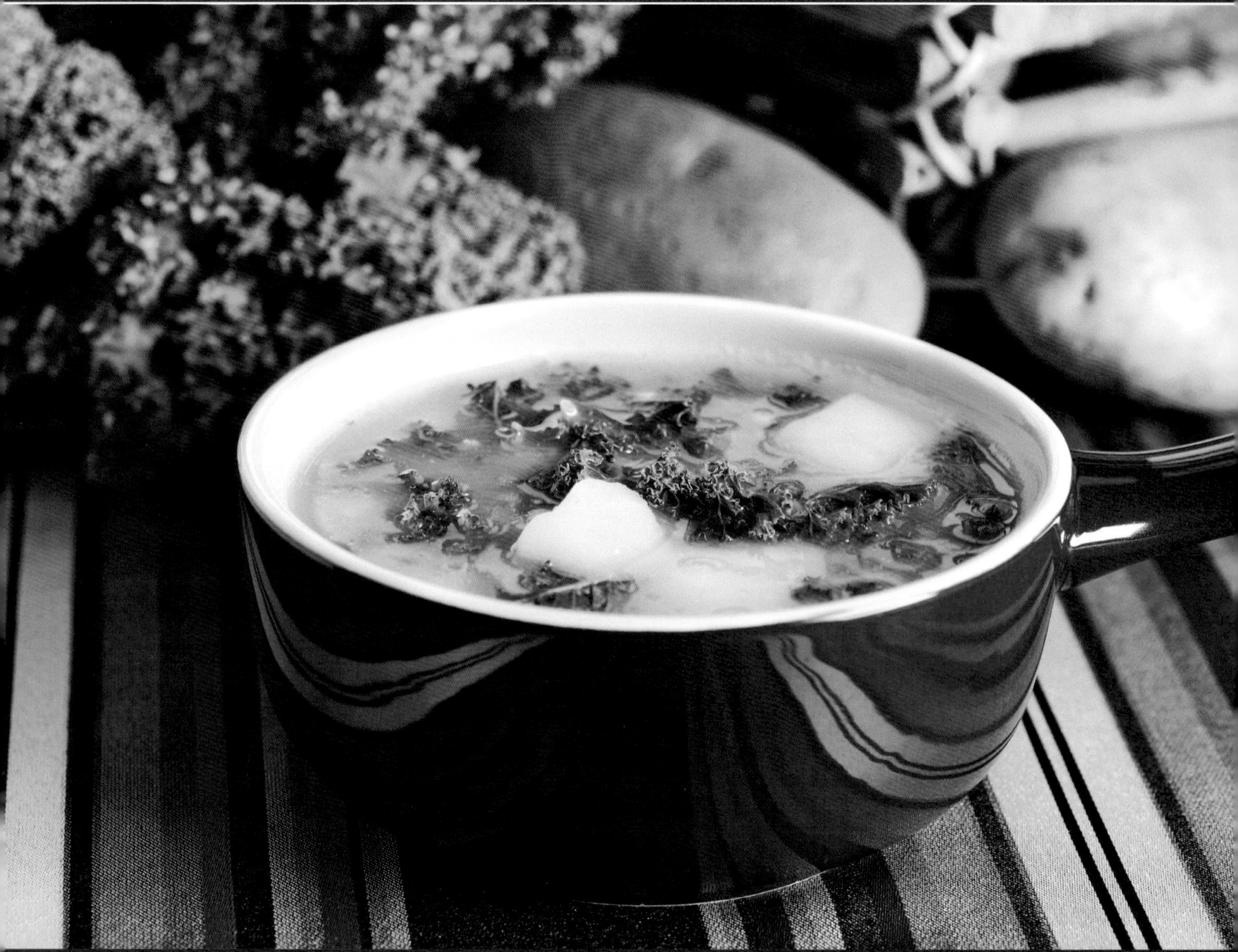

FOODTRIENTS

Fiber
Indoles
Isothiocyanates
Vitamin A
Vitamin C

Potato Kale Soup

This Balkan-inspired recipe has clean, bright flavors that go well together. Kale is an excellent source of vitamins A and C. It's also part of the cabbage family, so it has cancer-fighting compounds. If you can't find caraway powder, grind caraway seeds in a mortar and pestle, an electric spice grinder, or even a coffee grinder. For a milder version of this soup, omit the caraway and marjoram and season with sea salt and ground pepper.

1. Place the potatoes, salted water, caraway powder, garlic, and marjoram in a large saucepan or Dutch oven. Boil until potatoes are soft, about 15–20 minutes, skimming foam occasionally.

2. Stir in the cornstarch mixture and cook until the soup thickens slightly, about 1 minute.

3. Add the kale and cook until leaves are softened, about 5–10 minutes. If you like your kale a bit crunchy, cook it for only a few minutes. If you like it softer, cook it longer.

Serves 4

1 peeled and cubed Idaho potato or 2 rose potatoes

½ tsp. kosher salt dissolved in 4 cups water

½ tsp. caraway powder

1 tsp. chopped garlic

¼ tsp. dried marjoram

2 Tbs. cornstarch dissolved in ¼ cup cold water

2 cups chopped kale, stems removed

cell
booster

FOODTRIENTS

Carotenoids
Chlorophyll
Oleocanthal
Sulfur compounds
Vitamin C

Ai Ao DP IB MB

Stuffed Petite Peppers

I like to combine the nutty flavor of millet with Canadian bacon and chlorophyll-laced parsley to make a satisfying filling for these cute pepper appetizers. Millet is a protein-rich but underused whole grain. Gluten free, it can be cooked like rice and used in place of white rice in many recipes—simply use three parts water to one part grain.

1. Place the millet and water in a covered saucepan and bring to a boil. Reduce heat to medium and cook for 20–25 minutes. When fully cooked, fluff millet with fork and toss in 1 tsp. of the olive oil. Set aside.

2. Preheat oven to 400 degrees. In a food processor, mix the Canadian bacon and the parsley until the mixture resembles ground meat, about 1–2 minutes.

3. In a skillet, sauté the garlic and onion in the remaining 3 tsp. olive oil over medium-high heat until the onions are translucent, about 3–5 minutes. Add the Canadian bacon mixture and cook until browned, an additional 2–3 minutes.

4. In a bowl, combine millet, onion-bacon mixture, paprika, and egg white.

5. Halve the peppers lengthwise and stuff with millet-bacon mixture. Top with the panko breadcrumbs.

6. Bake peppers on a greased baking sheet at 400 degrees until browned, about 15 minutes.

Serves 4–6

½ cup millet

1 ½ cups water

4 tsp. olive oil

4 slices Canadian bacon

¼ cup chopped parsley

½ tsp. minced garlic

¼ cup chopped onion

¼ tsp. paprika

1 medium egg white

8–10 mini bell peppers, tops and seeds removed

¼ cup panko breadcrumbs

FOODTRIENTS

Oleocanthal
Omega-3s
Selenium
Zinc

Homemade Sardines

Sardines are any small fish—such as mackerel, smelt, or herring—that are preserved in oil or packed in sauce. Sardines are a good source of protein, iron, zinc, vitamin D, and calcium (if you eat the bones). I like to make my own at home because it's not very difficult and the results are wonderful. The sweet pickle juice adds a beautiful complexity while the olive oil provides the anti-inflammatory nutrients oleocanthal and oleuropein. I like to mash the sardines and eat them on crackers. You can also use larger fish, such as trout, cut into pieces. For a main course, see my Homemade Sardines with Tomatoes (page 91).

1. In a deep glass or ceramic dish, add the fish to the saltwater brine. Refrigerate, covered, for at least 3 hours.

2. Remove the fish from the brine. Add fish to a slow cooker with the remaining ingredients. Make sure the fish is completely covered with liquid. Add water if necessary.

3. Simmer on low heat until the fish is very soft, about 3–6 hours, depending on the size of the fish.

Serves 2–4

2–3 lb. small whole fish (mackerel, herring, or smelt), cleaned, heads removed, skin on, and bones in

¼ cup kosher salt dissolved in 2 cups water

¾ cup olive oil

¾ cup water

¾ cup pickle juice from a jar of sweet pickles

3 bay leaves

2 Tbs. peppercorns

age
defying

FOODTRIENTS

Choline
Fiber
Lutein
Potassium
Vitamin C

Grilled Artichokes with Moringa Dip

In this tasty appetizer, I pair moringa—which is loaded with protein, calcium, iron, vitamins A and C, and potassium—with artichokes, which add lutein and fiber. I like to steam the artichokes first and finish them on the grill, but you can omit this step to save time. Add other grilled vegetables such as red bell peppers, zucchini, and asparagus to expand on this delicious party food.

Serves 4–6

4 artichokes, trimmed and steamed for 30 minutes

2–3 Tbs. olive oil

1 cup olive oil mayonnaise

1 Tbs. finely chopped red onion

1 Tbs. finely chopped sweet pickles or sweet pickle relish

½ cup fresh moringa leaves or 1 tsp. moringa powder dissolved in 1 Tbs. warm water

Sea salt and ground pepper to taste

1. Preheat grill. Cut each steamed artichoke in half and remove the choke.

2. Brush each artichoke half with olive oil and grill over medium heat, cut side down, for 2 minutes. Set aside.

3. To make the moringa dip, combine the remaining ingredients in a small bowl and mix with a wooden spoon.

Salads

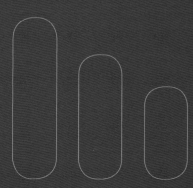

FOODTRIENTS

Carotenoids
Fiber
Quercetin
Resveratrol
Selenium
Sulfur compounds

Apple Barley Salad

Barley is a great source of fiber, B vitamins, and selenium. I serve it with apples in this bright, crunchy salad. For the corn kernels, I prefer fresh-roasted corn, but you can use thawed frozen corn kernels, too. The apples can be any variety or color that you like, or even a combination. All apples contain quercetin, a compound that helps support the immune system, thereby "keeping the doctor away." Raisins provide antioxidants and resveratrol, the same compound found in red wine. My Honey-Lime Dressing increases the antioxidant, anti-inflammatory, and immunity-boosting components of this recipe.

1. Rinse the barley in cold water to separate the grains.

2. In a large bowl, mix together the barley, corn, apples, scallions, carrot, and raisins. Season with the salt and pepper.

3. Toss with garlic-free Honey-Lime Dressing.

Serves 4–6

1 cup cooked barley

½ cup corn kernels

2 ⅔ cup chopped apples, peels on

2 Tbs. chopped scallions

½ cup shredded carrot

½ cup raisins

Sea salt and ground pepper to taste

1 recipe Honey-Lime Dressing (page 98), garlic omitted

body
rejuvenator

FOODTRIENTS

Carotenoids
Fiber
Oleocanthal
Potassium
Vitamin C

Beet and Potato Salad

This recipe is my take on the Russian version of potato salad. The wonderful deep-purple color of beets signifies the presence of helpful betalains, which are phytonutrients that support your body's detoxification systems. Beets are also a great source of folate and fiber. Potatoes are a good source of vitamin B6 and vitamin C.

1. Boil the beets in a large pot of salted water until tender, about 20–30 minutes. Drain, peel, and cut half the beets into ¼-inch cubes. Set aside. Cut remaining beets crosswise into slices and reserve for garnish.

2. Separately, boil the potatoes in a large pot of salted water until tender, about 20 minutes. Drain and place in a large bowl. Set aside.

3. Blanch the carrots and string beans in boiling salted water until crunchy and still colorful, about 3–5 minutes. Drain and plunge the vegetables into cold water to halt the cooking process and preserve the bright colors of the vegetables. Set aside.

4. To make the marinade, mix together the vinegar, sugar, salt, and pepper in a medium bowl.

5. Add the blanched carrots, string beans, cucumber, and three-quarters of the marinade to the potatoes and toss well. In a separate bowl, toss the cubed beets with the remaining marinade. Let everything stand for 20 minutes.

6. Drain the vegetables and potatoes and discard the marinade. Add the mayonnaise and stir to combine. Drain the beets.

7. To assemble, arrange beet slices on salad plates. Top with a ring of potato-vegetable mixture and cubed beets. Garnish with chopped eggs and olive slices.

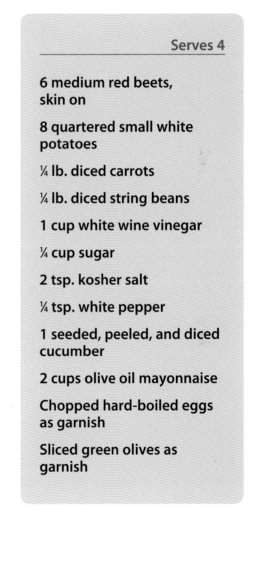

Serves 4

6 medium red beets, skin on

8 quartered small white potatoes

¼ lb. diced carrots

¼ lb. diced string beans

1 cup white wine vinegar

¼ cup sugar

2 tsp. kosher salt

¼ tsp. white pepper

1 seeded, peeled, and diced cucumber

2 cups olive oil mayonnaise

Chopped hard-boiled eggs as garnish

Sliced green olives as garnish

FOODTRIENTS

Allicin
Carotenoids
Choline
Fiber
Lutein
Lycopene
Oleocanthal
Potassium
Vitamin C

Bitter Melon Salad

Bitter melon, which resembles a wrinkly, light-green cucumber, is something of an acquired taste. Soaking it in salted water to remove the bitterness is the first step in getting people to fall in love with it. It's worth the trouble, because boiling bitter melon in water releases its antioxidant power. Bitter melon also has beta-carotene, potassium, and fiber. Asian herbalists prescribe it to diabetes patients to help them stabilize their blood sugar. This salad makes an excellent side dish for grilled meat, fish, and vegetables.

1. Slice the bitter melons lengthwise and remove all white parts, including the seeds. Sprinkle with the salt and let stand for 10–15 minutes. Rinse.

2. Cut the melons crosswise into strips. Blanch the slices in boiling water with the baking soda for 5 minutes. Drain and let cool.

3. To make the dressing, mix together the rice vinegar, olive oil, garlic, salt, and pepper. Let stand for up to 1 hour to allow the flavors to blend.

4. Toss the melon slices with the dressing.

5. To assemble, arrange the melon slices on salad plates. Top with the chopped eggs and tomatoes, evenly divided.

Serves 2–4

4 medium-size bitter melons

¼ cup kosher salt

Pinch of baking soda

1 cup seasoned rice vinegar

2 Tbs. extra-virgin olive oil

1 tsp. minced garlic

1 tsp. sea salt

¼ tsp. white pepper

2 chopped hard-boiled eggs

2 chopped medium tomatoes

graceful
aging

FOODTRIENTS

Carotenoids
Fiber
Lutein
Lycopene
Omega-3s
Potassium
Vitamin C

Spinach and Grapefruit Salad

Spinach contains iron as well as age-defying antioxidants. Grapefruit is chock-full of vitamin C and potassium. You can use pink or white grapefruit in this salad, though pink grapefruit has the added benefit of lycopene. If you use whole segments of the grapefruit, you'll also add fiber. The candied walnuts and dried apricots balance the acidity of the grapefruit and increase the antioxidants in this dish. My Tangy Ginger Dressing perfectly complements the mellow flavor of the spinach.

1. Wash and stem the spinach leaves and place in a bowl.

2. Add the grapefruit, walnuts, and apricots.

3. Toss with Tangy Ginger Dressing to taste.

Serves 2

1 bunch or 1 bag spinach leaves

1 whole grapefruit, segmented

¼ cup candied walnuts

¼ cup dried apricots

2 recipes Tangy Ginger Dressing (page 99)

SALADS

FOODTRIENTS

Anthocyanins
Carotenoids
Fiber
Potassium

Fig Salad

Figs are an excellent source of fiber. One serving of this salad provides about 12–15 percent of the daily requirement, in addition to some benefits from antioxidants, beta-carotene, and potassium. Figs also contain anthocyanins, which help reduce the risk of cancer. Deep purple figs have a greater concentration of anthocyanins than green or golden figs. Balsamic vinegar contains antioxidants and helps boost metabolism and regulate blood sugar. Slightly sweet and slightly tart, this salad also works well as an appetizer or dessert.

1. Drain the ricotta overnight in the refrigerator in a sieve lined with cheesecloth or a coffee filter.

2. Place the ricotta in a food processor and pulse a few times until smooth.

3. Combine the balsamic vinegar and water in a saucepan. Cook over low heat until thick and syrupy, about 20 minutes. Add the honey and stir until dissolved. Remove from heat to cool.

4. To assemble, place a few spoonfuls of ricotta cheese on each plate and spread out the cheese, making a bed for the figs. Distribute the figs among the plates. Sprinkle with the sea salt, drizzle with the balsamic syrup, and garnish with the mint leaves.

Serves 4–6

1 container (15 oz.) ricotta cheese

1 cup balsamic vinegar

½ cup water

1 Tbs. honey

10–12 quartered figs

Pinch of sea salt

Mint leaves as garnish

FOODTRIENTS

Carotenoids
Fiber
Indoles
Isothiocyanates
Oleocanthal
Resveratrol
Sulfur compounds
Vitamin C

Lentil Salad

Lentils contribute protein, fiber, and vitamin B6 to this hearty dish, making it both satisfying and energizing. The red cabbage, red wine vinegar, and leeks add a host of healthful benefits: anthocyanins, indoles, isothiocyanates, sulfur compounds, and resveratrol. You can also serve this delicious salad as a main course.

1. Place the lentils in a pot of boiling water and cook until al dente, about 20 minutes. They shouldn't be crunchy, but they shouldn't be too soft, either. Drain and set aside.

2. Heat 1 Tbs. of the olive oil in a small skillet over medium-high heat. Sauté the leek until opaque and soft, about 5–10 minutes.

3. To make the vinaigrette, place the remaining 4 Tbs. olive oil, red wine vinegar, mustard, shallot, salt, and pepper in a container with a tight-fitting lid. Shake well.

4. In a large bowl, combine the lentils, leek, cabbage, peppers, celery, and cucumber. Add half the vinaigrette and toss well. The salad will be slightly warm.

5. To serve, arrange over red cabbage or lettuce leaves with the remaining vinaigrette on the side.

Serves 2

1 cup dried green or black lentils

5 Tbs. extra-virgin olive oil

1 chopped leek (white part only)

¼ cup red wine vinegar

½ tsp. Dijon mustard

1 minced shallot

Sea salt and ground pepper to taste

½ cup shredded red cabbage

¼ cup diced yellow bell pepper

¼ cup diced red bell pepper

¼ cup diced celery

¼ cup seeded and diced cucumber

Red cabbage or lettuce leaves

body
rejuvenator

FOODTRIENTS

Allicin

Choline

Fiber

Indoles

Isothiocyanates

Lycopene

Oleocanthal

Potassium

Vitamin C

Ai Ao DP IB MB

Radish Salad

Radishes belong to the same family of vegetables as kale and cabbage and offer some of the same health-protecting benefits. I use the same simple oil-and-vinegar dressing here as on my Bitter Melon Salad (page 41), so both salads can be served together at a picnic or on a buffet.

Serves 2–4

2 daikon radishes or 1 bunch red radishes, stems removed

1 cup seasoned rice vinegar

2 Tbs. extra-virgin olive oil

1 tsp. minced garlic

1 tsp. sea salt

¼ tsp. white pepper

2 chopped hard-boiled eggs

6–8 sliced grape tomatoes

---

1. Slice the radishes very thinly using a food processor or mandoline.

2. To make the dressing, mix together the rice vinegar, olive oil, garlic, salt, and pepper. Let stand and allow the flavors to blend for up to 1 hour.

3. Toss the radishes with dressing.

4. To assemble, arrange the sliced radishes on salad plates. Top with the chopped eggs and tomato slices, evenly divided.

Main Courses

youth
serum

FOODTRIENTS

Allicin   Quercetin
Carotenoids   Sulfur compounds
Choline   Zinc
Lutein

Carrot Quiche

Carrots are well known for their beta-carotene content, which our bodies convert into vitamin A, a powerful antioxidant that is needed for healthy immune function. Carrots have hundreds of other carotenoids that help inhibit cancer growth. They also contain lutein, which is beneficial to eye health. Our bodies process the nutrients in carrots more efficiently when they are cooked. In this quiche, the carrots stay bright orange and firm, a nice contrast to the silky custard base.

1. Preheat oven to 450 degrees. Prick the pie crust with a fork and bake until just beginning to brown, about 7 minutes.

2. Heat the canola oil in a sauté pan over medium-high heat. Cook the bacon until it is golden brown.

3. Add the garlic, onion, and mushrooms and sauté until the onions are translucent, about 10 minutes.

4. Combine the egg substitute, half and half, evaporated milk, tapioca flour, salt, and pepper in a bowl and mix well.

5. Pour half of the egg mixture into the pie crust. Add the bacon mixture and the carrots. Pour in the remaining egg mixture.

6. Reduce oven temperature to 350 degrees and bake quiche until custard is set and crust is golden brown, about 30–45 minutes.

Serves 6–8

1 9-in. whole-wheat pie crust

2 tsp. canola oil

4 slices turkey bacon, chopped

2 tsp. chopped garlic

½ cup chopped onion

1 cup diced fresh mushrooms

1 cup egg substitute

½ cup half and half

½ cup fat-free evaporated milk

3 Tbs. tapioca flour

Sea salt and ground pepper to taste

2 cups shredded carrots

MAIN COURSES

FOODTRIENTS

Catechins
Fiber
Isoflavones
Omega-3s
Sulfur compounds

Green Tea Noodles with Edamame

Green tea, with its powerful theaflavins, is a strong antioxidant with vigorous anti-inflammatory properties. It's wonderful to drink on its own, but it also can be incorporated into recipes. An old Asian trick for adding more green tea to your diet is to boil soba, udon, or ramen noodles in green tea instead of water. These noodles need only 3–4 minutes to cook, so the green tea won't turn bitter. In addition, green tea has far more age-fighting power than water. If you want to eat these noodles cold, rinse them in cold water after draining and use cold edamame instead of hot. Hot or cold, my Tangy Ginger Dressing will keep the noodles from sticking and add extra flavor.

1. Bring the green tea to a boil in a small stockpot.

2. Add the soba noodles and cook for 3–4 minutes or according to package directions. Drain.

3. In a large bowl, toss the noodles with Tangy Ginger Dressing. Add the edamame and scallions.

4. To serve, divide between two bowls and garnish with sesame seeds.

Serves 2

2 cups brewed green tea

3 oz. soba noodles

1 recipe Tangy Ginger Dressing (page 99)

½ cup shelled cooked edamame (soybeans)

2 Tbs. chopped scallions

Black or white sesame seeds as garnish

MAIN COURSES

cell
power

FOODTRIENTS

Allicin
Carotenoids
Fiber
Gingerol

Indoles
Isoflavones
Isothiocyanates
Lutein

Tofu and Vegetable Stir-Fry

Tofu is an excellent alternative to meat, and this stir-fry will provide you with plenty of health-boosting vegetables. Broccoli is a good source of lutein, a hedge against macular degeneration. Cauliflower and kale have phytonutrients that protect against cancer. I use a wok to prepare this dish, but a large skillet will work, too. The tofu doesn't have to be fried first, but frying gives it a nice texture.

1. Drain the tofu and press between paper towels to remove excess water. Cut tofu into 1 to 1 ¼-inch cubes.

2. Heat 4 Tbs. of the peanut oil in a skillet over medium-high heat. Add the tofu and fry until golden brown, about 2–3 minutes. Remove tofu from pan and keep warm.

3. Add the remaining 2 Tbs. peanut oil to the pan and sauté the ginger and garlic over medium-high heat until lightly browned, about 2 minutes.

4. Add the carrots, snow peas, broccoli, and cauliflower and cook until just tender but still crunchy, about 7–10 minutes.

5. Add the kale and scallions and continue cooking until kale softens, about 4–5 minutes.

6. Stir in the oyster sauce mixture and cornstarch mixture and cook until a thick sauce forms, about 2 minutes. (If using unfried tofu, add now and cook until heated through, about 2–3 minutes.)

7. Remove vegetables from heat. Fold in tofu.

Serves 2–4

1 package (8 oz.) firm tofu

6 Tbs. peanut oil

1 Tbs. grated gingerroot

2 Tbs. minced garlic

1 cup baby carrots

1 cup snow peas

1 cup broccoli florets, cut or separated into bite-size pieces

1 cup cauliflower florets, cut or separated into bite-size pieces

3 cups chopped kale

2 chopped scallions

2 Tbs. oyster sauce combined with 2 Tbs. water

2 Tbs. cornstarch dissolved in ¼ cup cold water

MAIN COURSES

FOODTRIENTS

Allicin
Carotenoids
Choline
Gingerol

Indoles
Potassium
Vitamin E

Buckwheat Crepes

Full of fiber, vitamins, and minerals, buckwheat is a grain that is too often overlooked. Most people have never cooked with it or encountered it in restaurants. In this recipe, I turn buckwheat pancake mix into crepes and stuff them with healthful vegetables such as asparagus and immunity-boosting shiitake mushrooms.

1. To make the crepe batter, beat the eggs together with the salt and milk. Blend in the pancake mix until smooth. Let batter sit for 1 hour at room temperature.

2. To make the filling, heat the peanut oil in a large skillet over medium-high heat. Quickly sauté the garlic, ginger, and leeks for 2–3 minutes. Add the mushrooms, asparagus, and carrots and cook 3–5 minutes. Stir in the sesame oil, sugar, and soy sauce and cook for 2 minutes. Add the bok choy and remove skillet from heat. Stir in the jicama.

3. To make each crepe, coat a nonstick 9-inch crepe pan with cooking spray and place over medium heat. Pour ¼ cup batter into pan, rotating pan to distribute batter evenly. Cook until bottom of crepe is browned and batter is cooked through, about 3–4 minutes. Repeat to make additional crepes.

4. To make a homemade peanut sauce, combine ¾ cup water, 2 Tbs. soy sauce, 5 Tbs. peanut butter, and 3 Tbs. sugar in a saucepan and simmer until thick, about 5 minutes.

5. To assemble, lay each crepe on a serving platter. Lay about 1 cup of vegetable filling down the middle of each crepe and wrap crepe edges over vegetables. Drizzle crepes with peanut sauce.

Serves 4

2 medium eggs

Pinch of salt

1 cup low-fat milk

⅔ cup buckwheat pancake mix

3 Tbs. peanut oil

1 tsp. minced garlic

1 Tbs. grated gingerroot

½ cup chopped leeks (white part only)

1 cup chopped shiitake mushrooms

1 cup asparagus, thinly sliced into 2-inch strips

½ cup carrots, thinly sliced into 2-inch strips

1 tsp. sesame oil

2 tsp. sugar

2 Tbs. soy sauce

2 cups bok choy, thinly sliced into 2-inch strips

½ cup shredded jicama

Canola oil cooking spray

Peanut sauce (prepared or homemade)

MAIN COURSES

cellular
sensation

FOODTRIENTS

Allicin
Anthocyanins
Catechins
Selenium
Vitamin C

Summertime Grilled Chicken

This Mexican-inspired dish just screams "summer!" The chicken is marinated in my Honey-Lime Dressing, grilled, and paired with my refreshing Strawberry-Avocado Relish for an immunity boost, a dose of antioxidants, and detoxifying support. Serve with corn on the cob or tortillas.

1. Marinate the chicken breasts in the Honey-Lime Dressing in the refrigerator for at least 4 hours. The easiest way to ensure that the marinade coats the chicken evenly is to put both in a resealable plastic bag and squeeze the air out before sealing.

2. Remove chicken, reserving marinade. Prepare grill.

3. Grill the chicken breasts over medium-high heat until they are no longer pink in the middle, about 8–10 minutes per side. Baste with the reserved marinade while cooking.

4. To serve, arrange the chicken breasts on plates and spoon Strawberry-Avocado Relish over them.

Serves 2

3–4 lb. boneless, skinless chicken breasts

1 recipe Honey-Lime Dressing (page 98)

1 recipe Strawberry-Avocado Relish (page 104)

MAIN COURSES

immune
strengthening

FOODTRIENTS

Allicin
Choline
Lycopene
Oleocanthal

Quercetin
Selenium
Sulfur compounds

Mama's Chicken Sauté

My mother made this dish for our family dinners whenever we wanted comfort food. I always think of her when I make it. It has chicken and egg—symbols of the life cycle. I usually serve it over some form of potato: mashed, boiled, baked, or even fried (baked potatoes are the healthiest option). The chicken provides selenium, and the tomatoes offer lycopene. The garlic contributes healthy allicin compounds, while the olive oil adds natural anti-inflammatory compounds (oleocanthal and oleuropein).

1. Heat the olive oil in an enamel-coated cast-iron casserole or Dutch oven over medium-high heat. Add the garlic, onion, and tomatoes and sauté for about 5 minutes.

2. Add the chicken, soy sauce, bay leaves, and pepper. Bring to a boil, reduce heat, and simmer for 10–15 minutes.

3. Add the eggs and simmer until chicken is cooked through and sauce has thickened, about 10 minutes.

Serves 4

2 Tbs. olive oil

1 Tbs. minced garlic

½ cup diced onion

2 cups diced tomatoes

12 oz. skinless, boneless chicken breasts, cut into 2-inch strips

¼ cup soy sauce

2 bay leaves

Pinch of ground pepper

2 hard-boiled eggs

MAIN COURSES

FOODTRIENTS

Oleocanthal
Resveratrol
Selenium

Stuffed Turkey Rolls

I pack these turkey cutlets with my Savory Stuffing, roll them up, and secure them with kitchen twine. The finished rolls are sliced and fanned out on a plate to make a beautiful presentation. Because I marinate the turkey before cooking, it's juicy and flavorful. The selenium in turkey can increase your resistance to infection. The red wine (I use a Pinot Noir) adds a bit of resveratrol to the selenium's antioxidant power.

1. To make the marinade, combine the soy sauce, Worcestershire sauce, lemon juice, red wine, salt, and pepper in a large resealable plastic bag.

2. Add the turkey cutlets to the bag. Squeeze out the air, seal the bag, and marinate in the refrigerator for at least 30 minutes.

3. Remove cutlets, reserving the marinade. Pat each cutlet dry with paper towels.

4. On a work surface, lay one cutlet so it slightly overlaps a second one. Pound the seam together with a mallet. You should have one fairly large, thin turkey round. Repeat with the remaining cutlets until you have 3 rounds.

5. Spread about ½ cup of Savory Stuffing evenly onto each turkey round, smoothing almost to the edge. Roll up the turkey, pinwheel style, and secure with kitchen twine.

6. Heat the butter and olive oil in a heavy-bottomed sauté pan over medium-high heat. Add the turkey rolls and sear until a golden crust develops, about 1–2 minutes per side.

7. Preheat oven to 375 degrees. Place turkey rolls in a glass or ceramic baking dish. Spoon the reserved marinade and any remaining stuffing around the rolls. Cover with foil and bake until the turkey is cooked through, about 20–30 minutes.

8. Before serving, remove the twine and cut each turkey roll into 5 slices.

> Serves 6
>
> **¼ cup soy sauce**
>
> **2 tsp. Worcestershire sauce**
>
> **1 Tbs. lemon juice (about ½ lemon)**
>
> **2 Tbs. red wine**
>
> **Sea salt and ground pepper to taste**
>
> **6 turkey cutlets or butterflied turkey breasts**
>
> **1 recipe Savory Stuffing (page 102)**
>
> **2 Tbs. butter**
>
> **2 Tbs. olive oil**

MAIN COURSES

inflammation
fighter

FOODTRIENTS

Allicin   Quercetin
Curcumin   Selenium
Lauric acid   Sulfur compounds

Turkey in Turmeric Sauce

Turmeric, an anti-inflammatory, is a main ingredient in Indian curries. With its bright yellow color, turmeric pairs beautifully with poultry and fish. Its mild flavor goes well with garlic. Coconut milk has been much maligned for its saturated fat, but new research has revealed that its medium-chain fatty acids increase HDL, or "good" cholesterol, not LDL, or "bad" cholesterol. The fat in coconut milk supports the flavor of turmeric very well. For this recipe, I use only the thick liquid at the top of the can of coconut milk. To get double the turmeric benefits of this dish, serve it over my Turmeric Rice (page 103).

1. Heat the peanut oil in an enamel-coated cast-iron casserole or Dutch oven over medium-high heat. Add the garlic and onion and sauté until onions are translucent, about 5 minutes.

2. Add the turkey, fish sauce, turmeric, salt, and pepper. Cook for 5 minutes.

3. Add the water. Cover, reduce heat to medium, and cook until turkey is tender, about 20 minutes.

4. Add the thick part of the coconut milk to the pan and cook until the sauce is thick, about 5–10 minutes.

Serves 2–4

2 Tbs. peanut oil

1 Tbs. chopped garlic

½ cup chopped onion

2–3 lb. turkey breast, cut into medallions or thick strips

1 Tbs. fish sauce

2 tsp. turmeric powder or ½ cup Fresh Turmeric Juice (page 106)

Sea salt and ground pepper to taste

1 cup water

½ cup coconut milk, thick liquid only

MAIN COURSES

damage
reversing

FOODTRIENTS

Fiber
Gingerol
Omega-3s
Selenium
Sulfur compounds

Cornish Game Hen and Brown Rice Stew

This thick and hearty stew is my take on the classic Asian chicken soup. The brown rice makes it even healthier thanks to its high-fiber, selenium-rich properties. Feel free to add carrots, celery, or spinach to the mix. Add hard vegetables earlier in the cooking process and greens or herbs later. I like to soak the brown rice overnight before cooking it. This shortens the cooking time by about 20 minutes.

1. Smash the gingerroot with the side of a knife.

2. Heat the oil in an enamel-coated cast-iron casserole or Dutch oven over high heat. Sear the ginger until golden brown, about 1 minute.

3. Add the onion and the game hen and sear until the game hen is browned on all sides, about 5 minutes.

4. Add the water, garlic salt, and bouillon to the pot and bring to a boil over high heat. Cover, reduce heat, and simmer for 10 minutes.

5. Add the cooked brown rice and simmer, stirring occasionally, until stew is thick, about 40 minutes.

6. Remove the ginger and, if desired, the bones and skin of the game hen. Garnish with toasted garlic and sliced scallions.

Serves 4–8

1 inch peeled gingerroot

1 Tbs. canola oil

¼ cup chopped onion

1 whole Cornish game hen, cut into 8 pieces

5 cups water

1 Tbs. garlic salt

1 chicken bouillon cube

1 ½ cups cooked brown rice

Toasted garlic as garnish

Sliced scallions as garnish

MAIN COURSES

health
enhancing

FOODTRIENTS

Allicin   Selenium
Choline   Sulfur compounds
Lycopene   Vitamin C
Quercetin   Zinc

Whole-Wheat Pasta with Chicken Livers

Liver is the most abundant food source of vitamin A. It's also an excellent source of iron and zinc. As with other whole-grain foods, whole-wheat pasta has considerable amounts of healthful fats, protein, antioxidants, B vitamins, minerals, and fiber. You can serve this vitamin-enriched sauce over a variety of whole-wheat pasta shapes such as fusilli, rigatoni, shells, spaghetti, or linguini.

1. In a medium saucepan, poach the chicken livers in the salted water for 10 minutes. Drain and dice.

2. Heat the oil in a saucepan over medium-high heat. Add the onion and celery and sauté until onion is translucent, about 7 minutes.

3. Add the bell pepper and garlic and cook for 3 minutes.

4. Add the diced poached livers and marinara sauce and simmer for 10–15 minutes.

5. Remove from heat and stir in half the Parmesan cheese. Spoon sauce over the whole-wheat pasta and top with the remaining Parmesan.

Serves 4

1 lb. chicken livers

1 tsp. kosher salt dissolved in 2 cups water

2 Tbs. olive oil

1 cup chopped brown onion

2 cups chopped celery

1 cup seeded and chopped green bell pepper

2 Tbs. minced garlic

3 cups marinara sauce

1 lb. cooked whole-wheat pasta

¼ cup grated Parmesan cheese

MAIN COURSES

heart
healthy

FOODTRIENTS

Fiber
Omega-3s
Quercetin
Selenium

Sulfur compounds
Vitamin E
Zinc

Meatloaf with Flaxseed

This Middle Eastern–style meatloaf is actually a ground beef and pine nut filling between two layers of a seasoned meat paste. The nutty flavor of flaxseed combines well with grass-fed ground beef, which has more healthful Omega-3s and conjugated linoleic acids (CLAs, or healthful fats) than you'll find in grain-fed beef. Tomato paste gives this dish a lycopene lift. For a spicier meatloaf, use red pepper paste instead. I like to eat this dish drizzled with lemon juice to bring out all the flavors.

1. To make the meatloaf, place half of the ground beef in a food processor and mix to a paste. Refrigerate until needed in step 3.

2. In a large bowl, combine the flaxseeds, bulgur wheat, water, salt, and cumin. Let stand until all the water is absorbed, about 30 minutes. Set aside.

3. Preheat oven to 350 degrees. Combine the tomato paste and the flaxseed-bulgur mixture and mix thoroughly with your hands. Add the ground beef paste and mix thoroughly with your hands. If needed, add up to 5 Tbs. of water to achieve a smooth texture that hangs together and doesn't crumble.

4. To make the filling, heat the canola oil in a sauté pan over medium-high heat. Add the remaining ground beef, onion, salt, and pepper and cook until the meat is browned, about 7–10 minutes. Cool and fold in the pine nuts.

5. To assemble, spread half the meat-flax-seed-bulgur paste into a greased 9" x 11" baking dish, preferably a glass Pyrex pan. Add the ground beef and pine nut filling. Top with the remaining paste by making the paste into a very flat patty and laying it on top of the ground beef.

6. Cover pan with foil and bake at 350 degrees until meatloaf is well done, about 30 minutes. Remove foil and brown for 5–10 minutes.

7. To serve, cut meatloaf into 3-inch squares, sprinkle with flaxseeds, and garnish with lemon wedges.

Serves 4–8

1 lb. grass-fed ground beef, divided

½ cup flaxseeds

2 ½ cups bulgur wheat

2 cups water

1 ½ tsp. sea salt

1 Tbs. ground cumin

¼ cup tomato paste

Up to 5 Tbs. water

2 Tbs. canola oil

1 cup diced onion

Sea salt and ground pepper to taste

3 oz. pine nuts

Pinch of flaxseeds

Lemon wedges as garnish

MAIN COURSES

FOODTRIENTS

Choline
Lycopene
Quercetin
Sulfur compounds

Pork Loin Pockets

I spread pork tenderloin slices with tomato paste to give this dish the antioxidant benefits of lycopene. Canadian bacon has less fat than its American counterpart. It also adds a lot of flavor. Sulfur compounds in onions are great anticancer agents. Onions also contain antioxidants and quercetin. Steamed carrot sticks and broccoli make a nice accompaniment to these tasty pockets.

1. Preheat oven to 350 degrees.

2. Lay the pork tenderloin slices between sheets of plastic wrap and pound with a mallet into discs about ⅛-inch thick.

3. Season each round with the salt and pepper. Spread about 1 tsp. tomato paste over each round.

4. Lay a slice of Canadian bacon across half of each round and fold the remaining half over to form a pocket.

5. Dredge each pocket in flour, then dip in eggs. Dip in breadcrumbs, coating evenly.

6. Place pockets in a single layer in a greased baking dish. Brush tops with melted butter and scatter the onion and mushrooms over pockets.

7. Bake uncovered at 350 degrees until the pockets are cooked through and coating is golden brown, about 30–35 minutes.

> **Serves 6–8**
>
> **1 pork tenderloin (about 1 lb.), cut into 8 slices**
>
> **Sea salt and ground pepper to taste**
>
> **1 can (6 oz.) tomato paste**
>
> **8 slices Canadian bacon**
>
> **¼ cup flour**
>
> **2 beaten medium eggs**
>
> **1–2 cups breadcrumbs**
>
> **¼ cup melted butter**
>
> **1 cup sliced onion**
>
> **2 cans (4 oz. each) whole button mushrooms**

MAIN COURSES

body
energizer

FOODTRIENTS

Chlorophyll
Choline
Vitamin C
Zinc

Veal Meatballs with Parsley and Mushroom Gravy

The chlorophyll in fresh parsley gives this herb its antioxidant power, while vitamin C makes it a good anti-inflammatory. Parsley also contains folic acid, which is great for protecting your heart. I use a half cup of fresh parsley in these delicious meatballs, then sprinkle more on top when plating. I've included a quick gravy recipe that goes well with these parsley meatballs or over mashed potatoes.

1. Preheat oven to 400 degrees.

2. To make the meatballs, combine the first six ingredients in a large bowl. With your hands, shape mixture into about 24 medium-sized meatballs.

3. Heat the oil in a cast-iron skillet or grill pan over medium-high heat. Add meatballs and fry until brown on all sides, about 2 minutes per side.

4. Place meatballs in a shallow baking dish. Bake at 400 degrees until cooked through, about 10 minutes.

5. To make the mushroom gravy, combine the cream of mushroom soup, milk, parsley, Worcestershire sauce, and pepper in a medium saucepan. Cook over medium heat until heated through, about 7–10 minutes.

Serves 2–4

1 lb. ground veal

¼ cup chopped onion

2 medium eggs

Sea salt and ground pepper to taste

½ cup chopped parsley

2 Tbs. seasoned breadcrumbs

¼ cup canola oil

1 can (10.75 oz.) condensed cream of mushroom soup

¾ cup low-fat milk

2 Tbs. chopped parsley

1 Tbs. Worcestershire sauce

Pinch of ground pepper

MAIN COURSES

FOODTRIENTS

Allicin
Isothiocyanates
Selenium
Zinc

Spiced Rack of Lamb

Lamb and other red meat have vitamin B12 for energy and lysine for repairing tissue. Garlic's many compounds, including allicin, work in tandem to create a relaxing effect on artery walls, keeping them free of excess cholesterol and minimizing inflammation. I use garlic with black pepper and horseradish to spice up this rack of lamb. New Zealand lamb is lower in fat, cooks faster, and is more tender than American varieties such as Colorado lamb.

1. Preheat oven to 450 degrees.

2. Sprinkle the rack of lamb with the salt and pepper.

3. Sear the lamb, fat side down, in a large nonstick skillet over high heat until browned, about 3–5 minutes. Turn over and sear for 3 minutes. Remove from skillet and place in a roasting pan.

4. Mix the garlic and horseradish. Spread over the lamb.

5. In a small bowl, combine the rosemary, thyme, parsley, and breadcrumbs. Fold in the melted butter.

6. Pat the herb-breadcrumb mixture over the lamb and roast at 450 degrees for 10 minutes for rare, 12 minutes for medium rare, or 15 minutes for medium to well done.

Serves 6–8

New Zealand rack of lamb (about 1 lb.)

Sea salt and ground pepper to taste

1 tsp. minced garlic

2 Tbs. prepared horseradish

1–2 tsp. minced rosemary

1–2 tsp. minced thyme

1–2 tsp. minced parsley

1 cup seasoned breadcrumbs

1 Tbs. melted butter

MAIN COURSES

FOODTRIENTS

Isothiocyanates
Selenium
Sulfur compounds
Zinc

Mustard-Crusted Tri-Tip

Mustard is a highly popular and widely used condiment that has sparked interest among nutritionists. Its selenium and magnesium have anti-inflammatory properties and may help reduce blood pressure. Its phytonutrients seem to inhibit the growth of certain cancer cells. Mustard also stimulates the saliva glands, aiding in digestion. I like to use Dijon mustard for the crust on this tri-tip, but you can use any flavorful prepared mustard. As with all red meat, the lysine in the beef repairs tissue and helps skin build new collagen. I use grass-fed beef for its Omega-3s and other healthful fats.

1. Spread the Dijon mustard over the tri-tip and refrigerate overnight.

2. Preheat oven to 200 degrees. Remove the tri-tip from refrigerator. Sprinkle with the garlic salt and mesquite seasoning.

3. Bake at 200 degrees for 2 hours.

4. Turn up the heat to broil. Broil the roast until top is browned and sizzling, about 10 minutes.

5. Remove the roast from oven and allow it to sit for 30 minutes before slicing.

Serves 4–6

1 tri-tip (about 2–3 lb.) grass-fed beef roast

¼ cup Dijon mustard

3 Tbs. seasoned garlic salt

3 Tbs. sweet mesquite seasoning

MAIN COURSES

FOODTRIENTS

Carotenoids	Omega-3s
Fiber	Selenium
Indoles	Sulfur compounds
Isothiocyanates	Vitamin C
Oleocanthals	Zinc

Seafood with Wild Rice

This recipe combines seafood and wild rice to create a wholesome, flavorful, and filling one-dish meal. The Omega-3s in the seafood and wild rice smooth and soften the skin. For a variation, try adding chicken and sausage to your favorite seafood.

1. Place the rice in a bowl, cover with the water, and soak overnight. Drain.

2. Combine the chicken broth and rice in a saucepan and bring to a boil. Cook covered over low heat until all liquid is absorbed, about 30 minutes. Remove from heat and stir in 2 Tbs. of the olive oil. Set aside to cool.

3. Heat the remaining 2 Tbs. olive oil in a large skillet over medium-high heat. Add the onion, bay leaves, carrot, celery, broccoli, and peppers and cook for about 5 minutes. Add the seafood and cook for 10–12 minutes. Turn the seafood at least once during cooking. Season with the salt and pepper.

4. Add the rice to the skillet and cook until heated through, about 5 minutes.

MAIN COURSES

Serves 2

1 cup wild rice or a combination of wild and brown rice

4 cups water

2 cups chicken broth

4 Tbs. extra-virgin olive oil

¼ cup chopped onion

2 bay leaves

¼ cup chopped carrot

¼ cup chopped celery

¼ cup chopped broccoli

¼ cup chopped red bell pepper

¼ cup chopped yellow bell pepper

½ lb. seafood medley

Sea salt and ground pepper to taste

skin

calming

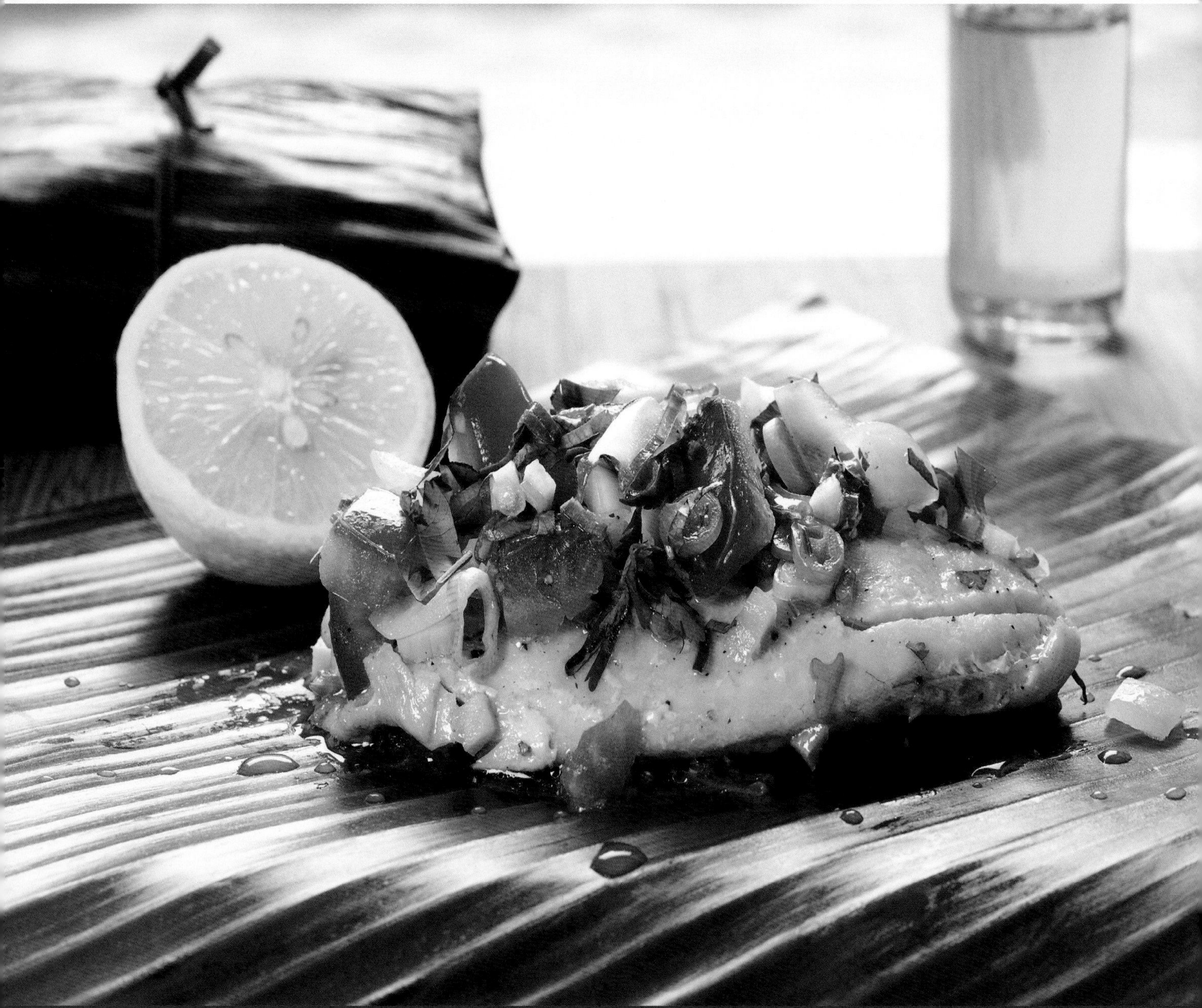

FOODTRIENTS

- Gingerol
- Lycopene
- Oleocanthals
- Omega-3s
- Vitamin C

Tilapia Fillets with Cilantro

The anti-inflammatory properties of fresh cilantro, ginger, and olive oil help keep skin looking young. I prefer to make this recipe using tilapia fillets, though you can substitute any firm, whitefish fillet. Using banana leaves to wrap the fillets will impart the full flavor of the fish, but the aluminum foil alone will also work.

1. Preheat grill or oven to 350 degrees. Lay a banana leaf on top of a large square of aluminum foil (about 8" x 8"). Place a fillet in the middle of the leaf. Repeat.

2. Add the salt and pepper and squeeze the juice from the lemon over the fillets.

3. Top the fillets with the tomato, ginger, onion, and scallions. Drizzle with the olive oil.

4. Wrap the banana leaves around the fillets to create a square packet. Wrap the packet with aluminum foil.

5. Bake fillets at 350 degrees for 13–15 minutes, or grill for 20 minutes on each side.

6. To serve, remove the aluminum foil wrap and transfer the fillets to a plate. Top packets with the cilantro and serve with the banana leaf.

Serves 2

2 banana leaves

2 tilapia fillets

Sea salt and ground pepper to taste

1 lemon, cut in half and seeds removed

½ cup seeded and sliced tomato

1 Tbs. peeled and thinly sliced gingerroot

¼ cup chopped onion

2 Tbs. chopped scallions

2 Tbs. olive oil

½ cup chopped fresh cilantro

FOODTRIENTS

Oleocanthals
Omega-3s
Selenium
Zinc

Baked Lobster Tails

Lobster not only tastes delicious, but its succulent flesh is loaded with Omega-3s, selenium, zinc, and B vitamins, which protect the brain and fight against cancer cells. The olive oil mayonnaise brings additional anti-inflammatory benefits while helping to prevent the tender lobster meat from drying out in the oven.

1. Preheat oven to 350 degrees.

2. Arrange the lobster tails shell side up on a cutting board. Using a sharp knife, split the top of the shell of each tail lengthwise. Loosen the lobster meat from the shells. Leave the meat inside the shells.

3. Sprinkle the tail meat with the salt, pepper, and lemon juice. Spread the mayonnaise over the meat and top with the Parmesan cheese.

4. Bake at 350 degrees until the shells are bright red and lobster meat is cooked, about 15 minutes. Garnish with lemon wedges and parsley.

Serves 2

2 lobster tails

Sea salt and ground pepper to taste

2 Tbs. lemon juice (about 1 lemon)

1–2 Tbs. olive oil mayonnaise

1 Tbs. grated Parmesan cheese

Lemon wedges as garnish

Chopped parsley as garnish

MAIN COURSES

FOODTRIENTS

Oleocanthals
Omega-3s
Selenium
Vitamin C

Grilled Swordfish in Secret Marinade

The secret to this dish is the oyster sauce in the marinade. For years, people have asked me what makes this swordfish so tangy and delicious. I've refused to divulge my secret... until now! The marinade makes the fish so flavorful that it doesn't need any extra sauce. But you can top it with my Papaya Salsa (page 100) for more antioxidant power.

1. In a small bowl, combine the oyster sauce, lemon juice, and olive oil.

2. Place the swordfish in a dish and pour the marinade over the fish. Cover and marinate in the refrigerator for 2 hours. Remove the fish and reserve marinade.

3. Preheat grill. Cook the swordfish over high heat, brushing with reserved marinade, for 5–7 minutes per side.

Serves 2

⅓ **cup oyster sauce**

¼ **cup lemon juice (about 2 lemons)**

¼ **cup olive oil**

2 swordfish steaks (about 6 oz. each)

MAIN COURSES

brains and
beauty

FOODTRIENTS

Oleocanthals
Omega-3s
Selenium

Home-Smoked Fish

This recipe uses a procedure that allows you to create smoked fish at home without using a smoker. Though it takes approximately 6 hours to brine, marinate, and bake the fish, it does not require considerable effort. The secret ingredient is hickory-flavored liquid smoke. Leaving the bones in the fish keeps it firm while it's "smoking."

1. Leave the fish whole or cut into 1-inch-thick steaks, skin and bones intact.

2. Place the fish and the saltwater brine in a large stockpot or bowl and soak in the refrigerator for 3 hours. Remove fish, drain, and pat dry. Discard brine.

3. Combine fish, olive oil, and liquid smoke in a large plastic container. Cover and place in the refrigerator overnight for a whole fish, 1 hour for steaks.

4. Preheat oven to 250 degrees. Bring fish to room temperature, reserving the marinade. Place fish directly on oven rack. On the rack below it, place a baking sheet lined with foil to catch fish drippings.

5. Bake fish at 250 degrees for 2 ½ hours, basting with the reserved marinade about every 20 minutes.

6. Increase temperature to 300 degrees and cook fish until the skin is golden brown and the flesh is firm, about 30 minutes.

7. Place fish on a platter and garnish with lemon slices. If desired, decorate platter with rock salt and fresh herbs.

Serves 4–6

4 lb. fresh trout, salmon, or mackerel, cleaned and gutted

1 cup kosher salt dissolved in 4 cups water

1 cup olive oil

¼ cup hickory-flavored liquid smoke

Lemon slices as garnish

Rock salt (optional)

Fresh herbs (optional)

MAIN COURSES

inflammation
fighter

FOODTRIENTS

Carotenoids   Omega-3s

Lycopene   Selenium

Oleocanthals   Zinc

Homemade Sardines with Tomatoes

It's hard to find a better health combination for your arteries than lycopene and Omega-3s. This recipe combines the power of tomatoes with delicious homemade sardines. Brining the fish makes all the difference, and cooking blends the fish and tomato flavors. I prefer to use small whole fish such as smelt, mackerel, or herring, which have a lower mercury content than larger fish. If you use a larger fish such as trout or tuna, cut it into pieces. I serve these tomato sardines over brown rice or combine them with mayonnaise, celery, onion, carrot, and jicama and make a sardine salad sandwich on crispy French bread.

1. Add the fish to the saltwater brine and refrigerate for at least 3 hours. Remove fish and discard the brine.

2. Place fish in a slow cooker with the olive oil and remaining ingredients. Be sure fish is completely covered with liquid. Add water if necessary.

3. Simmer on low heat until fish is very soft, even the bones, about 3–6 hours, depending on the size of the fish.

Serves 2–4

2–3 lb. small whole fish (mackerel, herring, or smelt), cleaned, heads removed, skin on, and bones in

¼ cup kosher salt dissolved in 2 cups water

¼ cup olive oil

1 can (15 oz.) tomato sauce

1 Tbs. tomato paste

1 cup water

3 bay leaves

1 clove garlic

2 tsp. peppercorns

1 tsp. salt

2 tsp. sugar

½ cup sliced sweet pickles

1 cup sliced carrots

FOODTRIENTS

Allicin   Quercetin
Carotenoids   Selenium
Gingerol   Vitamin C
Lauric acid   Zinc
Potassium

Shrimp and Moringa Curry

Shrimp and coconut milk are a classic Asian combination. I've added moringa powder to this very mild dish in order to increase the health benefits. If you want to dial up the heat a notch or two, use Serrano or other hot peppers in place of the mild red Anaheim chilies. If desired, serve over brown or jasmine rice.

1. Heat the peanut oil in a nonreactive saucepan, such as copper or enamel-coated cast iron, over medium-high heat. Add the garlic, ginger, and onion slices and sauté for 5 minutes.

2. Add the chilies and cook for 2 minutes.

3. Add the coconut milk, reduce heat, and simmer for 5 minutes.

4. Add the bell pepper, shrimp, salt, pepper, and moringa powder and simmer for 5 minutes.

Serves 2–4

¼ cup peanut oil

1 tsp. minced garlic

1 inch peeled and thinly sliced gingerroot

½ cup sliced red onion

2 red Anaheim chilies, seeded and cut into strips

1 can (19 oz.) coconut milk

1 orange or yellow bell pepper, seeded and cut into strips

1 lb. peeled tiger shrimp (devein, if desired)

Sea salt and ground pepper to taste

1 Tbs. moringa powder dissolved in 1 Tbs. warm water

MAIN COURSES

skin
preserving

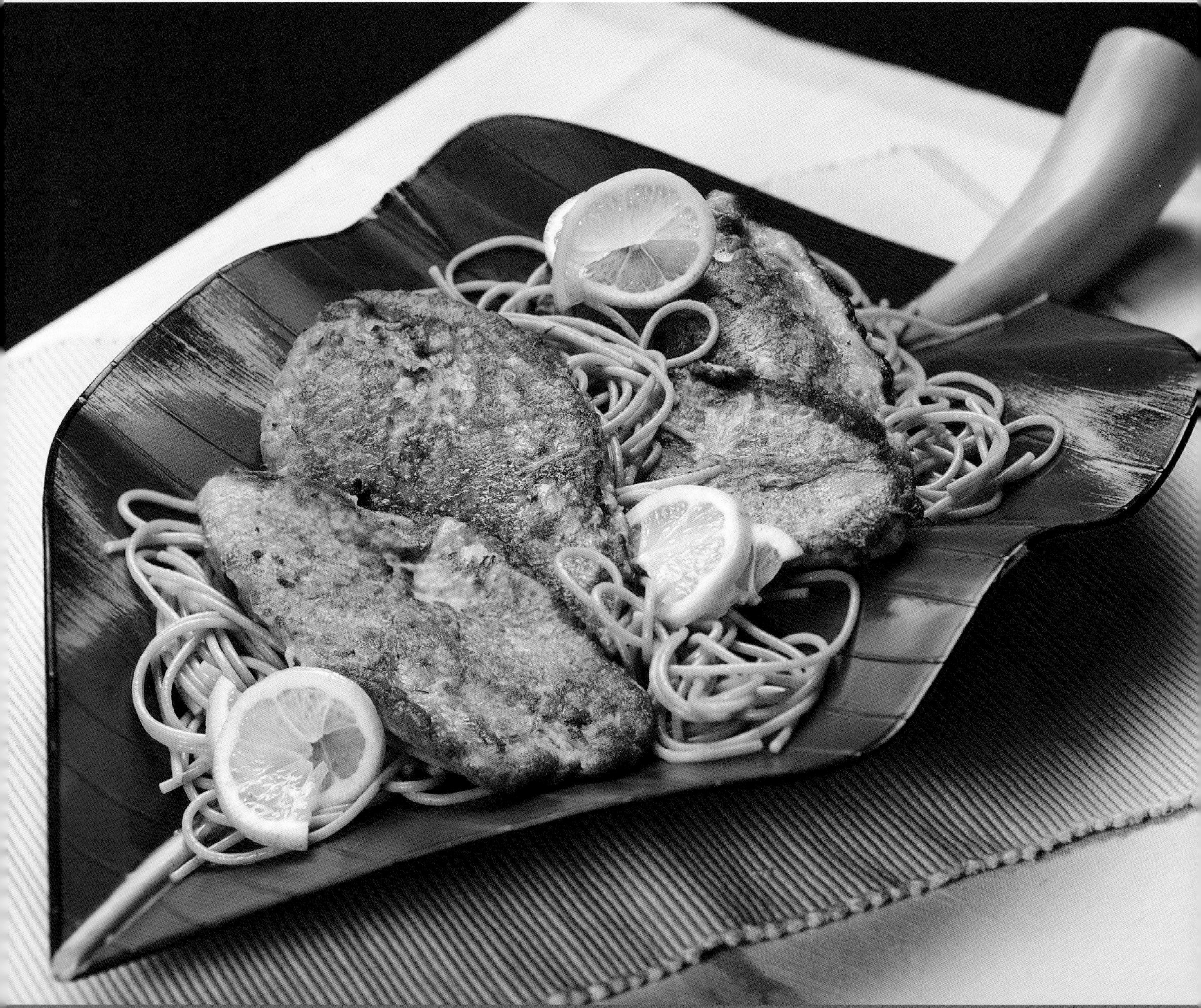

FOODTRIENTS

Choline
Curcumin
Oleocanthals
Omega-3s
Selenium

Whitefish with Turmeric

This is another of my cross-cultural wonders. It's like a veal scaloppini, but substituting fish for meat and marinating it in turmeric juice makes this dish much more healthful. The Omega-3s in the fish are great for skin hydration and elasticity, and turmeric is known the world over for its amazing anti-inflammatory benefits. Tilapia fillets work best because they're so thin and cook quickly, but you can use other thin whitefish fillets if you prefer. Serve these fillets over my Whole-Wheat Garlic Noodles (page 105).

1. To make the marinade, combine the turmeric juice, mirin, salt, and pepper in a small bowl.

2. Marinate the fillets in a covered dish in the refrigerator for 1 hour.

3. Drain fillets from marinade and set aside. Add the reserved marinade to the eggs. Stir to combine.

4. Dredge the fillets in the flour, then dip in the egg mixture.

5. Heat the olive oil in a large frying pan over medium-high heat. Add fillets and cook until golden brown, about 2–3 minutes on each side.

Serves 4

⅓ cup Fresh Turmeric Juice (page 106)

2 Tbs. mirin (seasoned rice wine)

Sea salt and ground pepper to taste

2 lb. tilapia fillets

3–4 beaten medium eggs

⅔ cup all-purpose flour

2–3 Tbs. olive oil

MAIN COURSES

FOODTRIENTS

Allicin
Lycopene
Oleocanthals
Quercetin
Selenium
Sulfur compounds

Shrimp in Tomato Sauce

Shrimp and tomatoes are a very Mediterranean combination. I use soy sauce in place of salt and add Worcestershire sauce to create a nice depth of flavor. You'll get selenium from the shrimp, allicin from the garlic, and lycopene from the tomatoes.

Serves 2

3 Tbs. olive oil

1 Tbs. chopped garlic

1 cup chopped onion

1 can (8 oz.) tomato sauce

2 tsp. soy sauce

2 tsp. Worcestershire sauce

¾ lb. peeled shrimp (devein, if desired)

Chopped parsley as garnish

Chopped chives as garnish

1. Heat the olive oil in a large skillet over medium-high heat. Add the garlic and sauté until it starts to turn golden brown, about 1–2 minutes.

2. Add the onion and cook until translucent, about 2–3 minutes.

3. Add the tomato sauce, soy sauce, and Worcestershire sauce and bring to a boil. Cover, reduce heat, and simmer for 10 minutes.

4. Add the shrimp and cook about 5–7 minutes.

5. To serve, spoon over white or brown rice and garnish with parsley and chives.

Extras

FOODTRIENTS

Allicin
Oleocanthals
Vitamin C

Honey-Lime Dressing

This is a very versatile dressing that you can toss with my Apple Barley Salad (page 37) or with any mixed greens. The lime juice provides vitamin C, while compounds in the chili powder help to neutralize free radicals in your cells. If you want a spicier dresssing, add cayenne pepper or red pepper flakes. Both contain capsaicin, which stimulates circulation. This dressing makes the perfect marinade for my Summertime Grilled Chicken (page 59). The lime brings out the flavor of the poultry, and the olive oil keeps it from sticking to the grill. To use this dressing with fruit salad, simply omit the allicin-rich garlic—it will still be nutritious!

Yields about ¼ cup

1 ½ Tbs. lime juice (about 1 lime)

1 ½ Tbs. honey

1 Tbs. extra-virgin olive oil

1 minced garlic clove

½ tsp. chili powder

Sea salt to taste

Combine all the ingredients in a container with a tight-fitting lid and shake until well blended.

good
digestion

FOODTRIENTS

Gingerol
Isoflavones

Tangy Ginger Dressing

Ginger gives this dressing its flavor as well as amazing anti-inflammatory benefits and pain-reducing effects. It also relaxes muscles, increases circulation, and aids digestion. Buy the whole gingerroot, then peel or cut off about an inch of the rough skin. Grate only as much ginger as you need, and put the root back into the refrigerator, ready to be peeled and grated for the next dish. I use this dressing with my Green Tea Noodles with Edamame (page 53) and over my Spinach and Grapefruit Salad (page 43). It works well with any mixed green salad.

Yields about ¼ cup

1 Tbs. grated gingerroot

1 Tbs. soy sauce

1 Tbs. mirin (seasoned rice wine)

1 Tbs. sesame oil

Dash of pepper

Combine all the ingredients in a container with a tight-fitting lid and shake until well blended.

EXTRAS

FOODTRIENTS

Carotenoids
Lutein
Vitamin C

Papaya Salsa

This refreshing relish will help boost your immune system and keep your skin young and elastic. Papaya is rich in vitamin C and beta-carotene, which your body converts to vitamin A. It's also high in potassium. Certain enzymes in papaya aid digestion. I use this salsa on grilled meats and fish, such as my Grilled Swordfish in Secret Marinade (page 87), and it's also delicious as an appetizer with whole-grain chips.

Yields about 4 cups

2 cups cubed papaya, ripe but still firm

¼ cup seeded and chopped red bell pepper

¼ cup chopped red onion

1 tsp. minced garlic

½ cup chopped fresh cilantro

½ tsp. seeded and chopped jalapeño pepper (optional)

2 Tbs. lime juice (about 1 lime)

2 Tbs. lemon juice (about 1 lemon)

1 tsp. red wine vinegar

Sea salt and ground pepper to taste

Combine all the ingredients in a large bowl and mix well with a wooden spoon.

immunity
boosting

FOODTRIENTS

Anthocyanins
Resveratrol
Vitamin C

Cranberry Compote

Cranberries are high in antioxidants and vitamin C. They even have a bit of resveratrol in them—the heart-friendly nutrient found in red wine. This recipe will keep for many days in the refrigerator. I use it in my Cranberry Bread Pudding (page 109) and on its own as an accompaniment for poultry.

Yields about 4 cups

¼ **cup water**

1 cup Whey Low Gold brown sugar substitute

1 cup fresh cranberries

1. Boil the water and sugar substitute in a large nonreactive saucepan, such as copper or enamel-coated cast iron, for about 5 minutes.

2. Add the cranberries and boil until most of the cranberries have softened and the sauce is thick, about 25 minutes.

3. Cool and refrigerate.

EXTRAS

energy booster

FOODTRIENTS

Oleocanthals
Quercetin
Sulfur compounds

Ai Ao DP MB

Savory Stuffing

I use this stuffing for my Stuffed Turkey Rolls (page 63). Homemade croutons, raw celery, and sausages give this dish its unique flavor and texture. To serve as a side dish, spread the stuffing in a greased baking dish and bake at 400 degrees for 20 minutes.

Yields 2–3 cups

4 Tbs. olive oil

½ cup chopped onion

½ lb. ground turkey

2 slices cubed whole-wheat bread

Sea salt and ground pepper to taste

½ tsp. Italian seasoning

1 cup turkey or chicken broth

¼ cup chopped celery

1 can (5 oz.) mashed Chicken Vienna sausages (optional)

1. Heat 3 Tbs. of the olive oil in a large pan over medium-high heat. Add the onion and cook until translucent, about 5 minutes.

2. Add the ground turkey and cook until done. Set aside.

3. To make the croutons, preheat oven to 350 degrees. Season the bread cubes with the salt and pepper, drizzle with the remaining 1 Tbs. olive oil and the Italian seasoning, and bake at 350 degrees for about 10–15 minutes.

4. Add the broth, croutons, celery, and sausages, if using, to the turkey mixture and mix well. Season to taste.

inflammation
fighter

Ai **Ao** **DP**

FOODTRIENTS

Curcumin

Turmeric Rice

This rice is mildly spiced because it's designed to go with my Turkey in Turmeric Sauce (page 65). If you want the rice to carry most of the flavor, substitute coconut milk for half of the water. Then serve it with grilled turkey, chicken, or fish. Either way, you get both anti-inflammatory and antioxidant benefits from the fresh turmeric.

Yields 2 cups

1 cup jasmine rice

½ cup Fresh Turmeric Juice (page 106), or 1 tsp. turmeric powder

2 cups water

---

1. Rinse the rice under running water once. Drain and set aside.

2. Combine the turmeric juice or powder with water in a large saucepan.

3. Add the rice to the turmeric water and bring to a boil. Cover, reduce heat, and simmer for 20 minutes.

EXTRAS

age
defying

FOODTRIENTS

Anthocyanins
Omega-3s
Vitamin C

Strawberry-Avocado Relish

No cooking is required for this condiment. The strawberries, avocado, and cilantro all contain antioxidants. Strawberries are also very high in vitamin C and flavonoids, while avocados also provide glutathione, a detoxifying agent. I use this relish with my Summertime Grilled Chicken (page 59), but it also makes a great topping for grilled fish and a satisfying dip for whole-grain tortilla chips.

Yields about 2 cups

1 ½ cups diced strawberries

1 diced medium-size avocado

¼ cup minced red onion

¼ cup lime juice (about 2 limes)

1 Tbs. chopped cilantro

1 tsp. sugar

Sea salt and ground pepper to taste

Combine all the ingredients in a bowl and mix well with a wooden spoon.

cellular
sensation

FOODTRIENTS

Allicin
Fiber
Oleocanthals
Selenium

Whole-Wheat
Garlic Noodles

This is basically an *aglio e olio* (garlic and oil) recipe made more healthful with whole-wheat pasta, which ensures you get fiber and selenium. The garlic and olive oil provide anticancer and anti-inflammatory benefits. I serve these noodles with my Whitefish with Turmeric (page 95).

Serves 2–4

6 cups water

1 tsp. salt

½ tsp. garlic powder

½ lb. whole-wheat noodles

2 Tbs. olive oil

2 Tbs. chopped garlic

1. Boil the water in a large stockpot with the salt and garlic powder.

2. Add the noodles and cook to desired tenderness. Drain and set aside.

3. Heat the olive oil in a sauté pan over medium-high heat. Add the garlic and cook until golden brown, about 2–3 minutes.

4. Add the noodles to the pan and toss until coated and heated through.

EXTRAS

inflammation
fighter

FOODTRIENTS

Curcumin

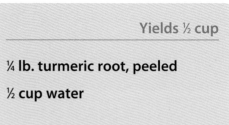

Fresh Turmeric Juice

Fresh turmeric root fights inflammation and contains antioxidants. The best way to enjoy fresh turmeric is to juice it. Once juiced and strained, it can be stored in a tightly closed container in the refrigerator for up to a week. I use it in my Turmeric Rice (page 103) and Turkey in Turmeric Sauce (page 65).

Yields ½ cup

¼ lb. turmeric root, peeled

½ cup water

1. Slice the turmeric root until it measures about 1 cup.

2. Place the turmeric slices in a food processor or blender. Add a bit of the water and blend at low speed. Gradually increase speed, slowly adding water until all of the water is used up and mixture is smooth.

3. Strain the juice using a fine-mesh strainer, cheesecloth, or coffee filter.

Desserts

disease
defying

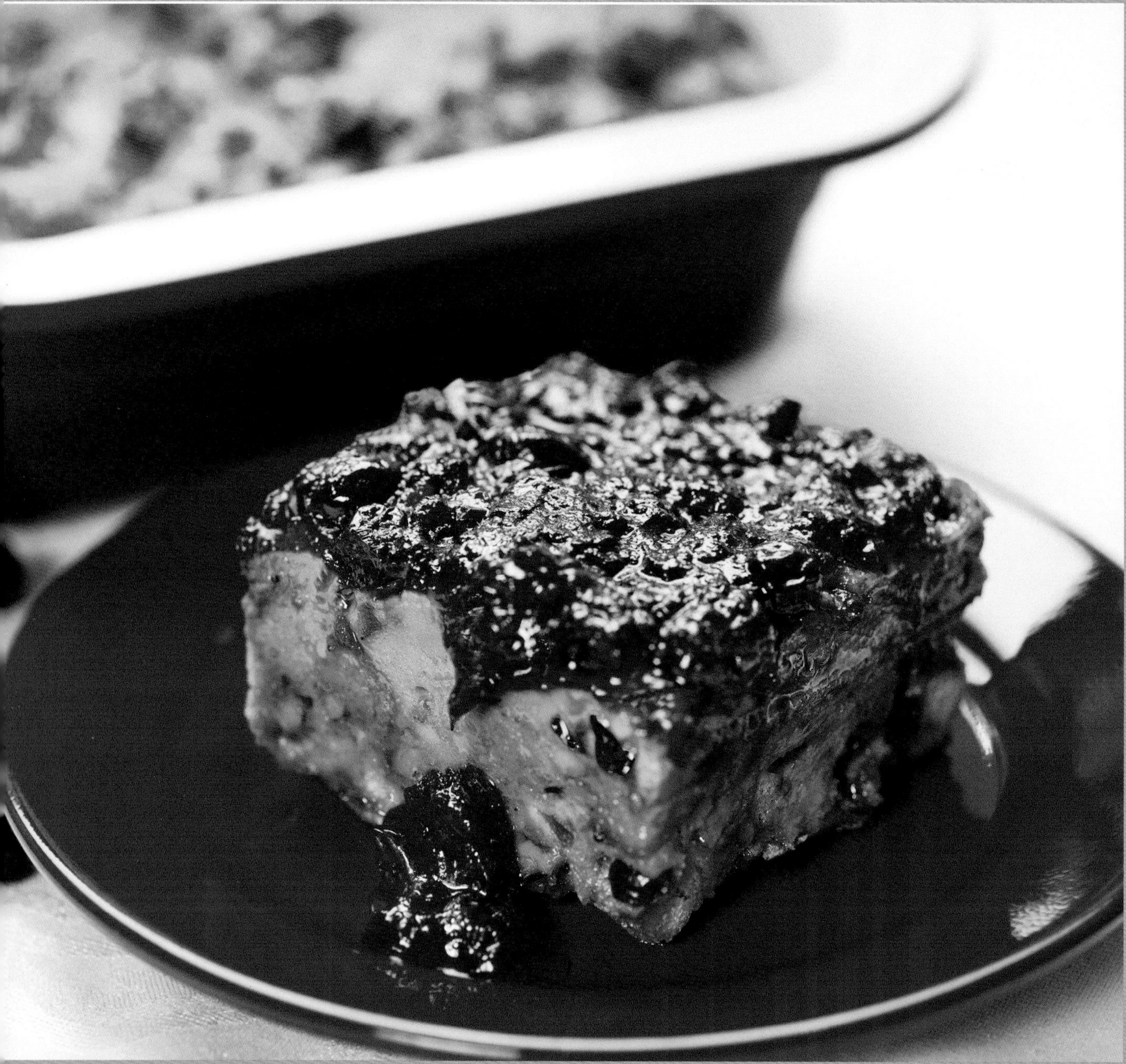

FOODTRIENTS

- Anthocyanins
- Choline
- Omega-3s
- Resveratrol
- Vitamin C

Cranberry Bread Pudding

Cranberries don't grow in the subtropical climate of Southeast Asia, so when my mother and I wanted to make this dessert, we had to use a local red-colored berry as a substitute. I like this recipe better with cranberries, which are high in vitamin C. They also rank very high on the oxygen radical absorbance capacity (ORAC) scale. Use my Cranberry Compote on the bottom layer (it becomes the top layer when you turn out the dessert). To serve this dessert cold, place the pudding in the refrigerator overnight before turning upside down.

1. Preheat oven to 350 degrees.

2. In a bowl, combine the eggs, the cubed bread, and the milk. Mix well and soak for 10 minutes.

3. Fold in the melted butter substitute, sugar substitute, walnuts, cranberries, and lemon zest.

4. Grease the sides of a loaf pan and spoon 1 cup of Cranberry Compote into the pan. Spoon the bread mixture over the compote.

5. Cover the pan with aluminum foil and place it in a larger roasting pan. Fill the roasting pan halfway with water. Bake at 350 degrees for 50 minutes.

6. Remove the foil and bake until top is golden brown and center is set, about 15 minutes.

7. Remove from oven and let cool for about 15 minutes. Turn the pudding out onto a serving platter for slicing. The compote will be on top, glistening and warm.

Serves 6–8

2 large beaten eggs

3 cups cubed whole-wheat bread

1 can (12 oz.) fat-free evaporated milk

¼ cup melted Smart Balance 50/50 Butter Blend

¼ cup Whey Low® Gold brown sugar substitute

¼ cup chopped walnuts

¼ cup dried cranberries

½ tsp. lemon zest

1 recipe Cranberry Compote (page 101)

DESSERTS

age
defying

FOODTRIENTS

Anthocyanins   Potassium
Choline   Vitamin C
Fiber   Vitamin E
Omega-3s

Prune and Walnut Bars

Prunes and walnuts are both exceedingly high in antioxidant power. Both are listed by the U.S. Department of Agriculture on the ORAC (oxygen radical absorbance capacity) scale with over 10,000 units. Prunes are also a great source of vitamin C. I've combined these two age-defying powerhouses into one great dessert.

1. Preheat oven to 325 degrees.

2. In a bowl, combine the white rice flour, tapioca flour, baking soda, baking powder, and salt. Add the prunes and walnuts. Mix well and set aside.

3. In a stand mixer or using beaters, cream the butter substitute until fluffy. Add the coconut butter and sugar substitute a little at a time.

4. Separately combine the eggs and egg substitute and whisk until smooth. Add to the creamed butter mixture.

5. Combine the creamed butter-egg mixture with the dry flour mixture.

6. Spread into a greased and floured 8"x 8" baking pan and bake at 325 degrees until the center is firm, about 40–45 minutes.

7. Cool for 15–20 minutes before cutting and serving.

Serves 8–10

¾ cup white rice flour

½ cup tapioca flour

1 tsp. baking soda

½ tsp. baking powder

¼ tsp. salt

1 cup chopped prunes

1 cup chopped walnuts

¾ cup Smart Balance 50/50 Butter Blend, softened

2 Tbs. coconut butter

1 ¼ cup Whey Low® Gold brown sugar substitute

2 large eggs

½ cup egg substitute

cellular
sensation

FOODTRIENTS

Anthocyanins
Catechins
Vitamin C

Almond-Blueberry Gelatin Parfaits

The flavors and colors of the almond and blueberry gelatins play off each other beautifully in this dessert. Blueberries rank very high in their ability to fight free oxygen radicals that damage cells. They also contain vitamin C and antibacterial elements called anthocyanosides, which are great for maintaining vein health. Almond milk is an excellent source of antioxidants.

1. To make the blueberry gelatin, combine the blueberry juice and 2 envelopes of gelatin in a double boiler and cook over medium-high heat until the gelatin is completely dissolved. Remove from heat.

2. Add the sugar, the lemon zest, and the chopped blueberries and mix well until the sugar is dissolved. Cool at room temperature.

3. Pour or ladle the blueberry gelatin mixture into 6 parfait glasses. Chill for 1–2 hours.

4. To make the almond gelatin, combine the almond milk and the gelatin in a double boiler and cook over medium-high heat until the gelatin is completely dissolved. Remove from heat.

5. Add the sugar and the almond extract and mix well until the sugar is dissolved. Cool at room temperature.

6. To assemble, pour or ladle the almond gelatin over the chilled blueberry gelatin parfaits. Return parfait glasses to the refrigerator and chill for 3 hours or overnight. Garnish with fresh blueberries.

Serves 6

2 cups blueberry juice

2 envelopes (1 oz. each) unflavored gelatin

¼ cup brown sugar

1 tsp. lemon zest

½ cup chopped fresh blueberries

2 cups almond milk

2 envelopes (1 oz. each) unflavored gelatin

¼ cup brown sugar

1 tsp. almond extract

Fresh blueberries as garnish

DESSERTS

nutrient
rich

FOODTRIENTS

Choline
Omega-3s
Selenium
Vitamin E

Brazil Nut Tarts

These tarts, with their hint of lime and rich texture, take Brazil nuts to a new level. Brazil nuts are full of selenium and protein, as well as Omega-3s, which help to keep your skin elastic and hydrated and to reduce swelling and redness. I like to make several small tarts from this recipe, but you can make one large tart if you prefer—just increase the baking time by 10–15 minutes.

1. Preheat oven to 350 degrees.

2. Line four 5-inch tart shells with the pie crusts. Poke the crusts with a fork and bake until just beginning to brown, about 10–15 minutes. Remove from oven and set aside.

3. In a bowl, combine the evaporated milk, diluted tapioca flour, and the eggs. Whisk together until smooth.

4. Cook the tapioca mixture in a double boiler over medium-high heat, stirring constantly, until thick, about 20–25 minutes.

5. Add the coconut butter, lime juice and zest, and sugar substitute and continue cooking and stirring for 10–15 minutes. Remove from heat and stir in the nuts.

6. Pour the mixture into the precooked tart pans and bake at 350 degrees until firm and golden brown, about 20–25 minutes.

Serves 4–8

2 9-in. whole-wheat pie crusts

1 can (12 oz.) fat-free evaporated milk

2 Tbs. tapioca flour diluted in 4 Tbs. water

2 beaten large eggs

2 Tbs. coconut butter

2 Tbs. lime juice (about 1 lime)

1 tsp. lime zest

½ cup Whey Low® Gold brown sugar subsitute

1 cup toasted and finely chopped Brazil nuts

DESSERTS

skin
strengthening

FOODTRIENTS

Anthocyanins
Isoflavones
Omega-3s
Vitamin C

Strawberry Tofu

Tofu is the perfect food to combine with fruit. Its texture is very pudding-like, similar to that of panna cotta. And because it has almost no taste, the full flavor of the fruit remains intact. Strawberries are high in vitamin C, which helps build collagen to strengthen the skin, and disease-fighting flavonoids.

1. To make the strawberry syrup, boil the water and sugar substitute in a nonreactive saucepan, such as copper or enamel-coated cast iron, until thick but not caramel, about 7 minutes. Add the diced strawberries and cook over low heat for 5 minutes. The pectin in the strawberries will thicken the syrup without the need to cook it further.

2. Remove syrup from heat and chill in refrigerator for at least 1 hour.

3. Line the sides and bottoms of four small glass bowls with the sliced strawberries.

4. Drain the tofu and press between paper towels to remove excess water. In a blender or food processor, mix the tofu until the texture is smooth, about 1 minute. Chill.

5. Spoon the tofu over the strawberry slices. Tap the bowls on the counter to break up any air pockets.

6. Pour the strawberry syrup over the tofu before serving.

Serves 4

¾ cup water

2 cups Whey Low® Gold brown sugar substitute

2 cups diced strawberries

1 cup thinly sliced strawberries

1 container (12.5 oz.) fresh silken tofu

DESSERTS

body
stabilizing

FOODTRIENTS

Catechins
Fiber
Lauric acid
Omega-3s

Chia Seed Treat

Chia seeds carry more Omega-3s than flaxseeds do, so they're a great anti-inflammatory and can help reduce bad cholesterol. There is some evidence that they can stabilize blood sugar levels, too. Chia seeds are either white or black and have a mild, nutlike flavor. I prefer the white seeds over the black. Chia seeds don't need to be cooked. Simply soak them in water for an hour to allow them to release their natural gelatin-like coating.

1. Combine the moringa powder, ⅔ cup of the water, and the coconut milk in a nonreactive saucepan, such as copper or enamel-coated cast iron. Bring to a boil, reduce heat, and simmer for 3 minutes.

2. In a large bowl, sprinkle the gelatin over the cold water and add the granulated sugar. Whisk together.

3. Add the hot moringa mixture to the gelatin and stir to combine. Refrigerate until set, about 2 hours.

4. Boil the brown sugar in 1 cup water until sugar is dissolved, about 5 minutes. Chill.

5. In a bowl, soak the chia seeds in 2 cups water for 1 hour. Chill.

6. To assemble, cut chilled gelatin into cubes and place in four dessert bowls. Pour green tea over cubes. Add a few tablespoons of the chilled brown sugar syrup to each bowl. Divide chia seeds evenly among bowls. Top with crushed ice.

Serves 4

½ tsp. moringa powder

3 ⅔ cups water

⅓ cup coconut milk

4 envelopes (1 oz. each) unflavored gelatin

⅓ cup cold water

2 Tbs. granulated (white) sugar

5 Tbs. brown sugar

⅓ cup white chia seeds

2 cups chilled green tea

Crushed ice

DESSERTS

FOODTRIENTS

Carotenoids
Fiber
Vitamin C

Mango Tapioca

A variation on traditional tapioca pudding, this refreshing dessert is low in fat but creamy and satisfying all the same. Mango contains skin-friendly carotenoids and vitamin C to help skin stay looking young. It also has silica, a mineral that keeps skin elastic by helping to form collagen.

1. Place the mango puree in a nonreactive saucepan, such as copper or enamel-coated cast iron. Add the lemon juice and sugar and cook over low heat, stirring constantly, until very thick, about 5 minutes.

2. Add the lemon zest, remove from heat, and set aside to cool. Reserve ½ cup of the mango mixture for the topping.

3. Place the tapioca and water in a small saucepan over medium-high heat and cook tapioca, stirring continuously, until it is thick and transparent, about 1–3 minutes.

4. Add the tapioca to the mango mixture. Fold in the evaporated milk.

5. Spoon the mango tapioca into martini glasses or parfait cups. Refrigerate overnight until set. Top with the reserved mango mixture or slices of fresh mangoes.

Serves 6–8

2 cups pureed mango

1 Tbs. lemon juice (about ½ lemon)

½ cup sugar

1 tsp. lemon zest

¼ cup tapioca

2 cups water

1 cup evaporated milk

DESSERTS

cell
booster

FOODTRIENTS

Quercetin
Vitamin E
Zinc

Pear and Apple Tart

In this dessert, I take the recipe for the classic French dessert *tarte tatin*—with its quercetin-containing apples—and add pears for their copper content and pecans and cinnamon, which are high in antioxidants. It is worth noting that when used in sufficient amounts, cinnamon also has anti-blood-clotting agents and anti-inflammatory properties and may help stabilize blood sugar levels.

1. Preheat oven to 425 degrees.

2. In a cold 8-inch cast-iron skillet, lay ½ of the butter pieces, evenly spaced. Sprinkle ½ of the sugar mixture over the pan. Lay the fruit, cut side up, over the butter and sugar, covering the entire pan. Pack the fruit tightly to avoid shrinking during cooking.

3. Squeeze the juice from the lemon over the fruit. Sprinkle the remaining ½ of the sugar mixture over the fruit. Dot with the remaining butter.

4. Place the skillet over medium-high heat and cook the fruit mixture until the butter melts and the sugar caramelizes, about 20 minutes. If hot spots develop, rotate the pan but do not stir the fruit.

5. Remove pan from heat and sprinkle the pecans over the fruit.

6. Top with the pie crust, folding edges into the pan so no crust is hanging over. Bake at 425 degrees until the pastry is golden brown, about 20–25 minutes.

7. Cool the pie until the caramel thickens without sticking to the pan, about 10 minutes. Turn out onto a plate before cutting and serving.

Serves 6–8

6 Tbs. butter, cut into small pieces

½ cup sugar, combined with ½ tsp. ground cinnamon

4 apples (Braeburn, Granny Smith, Gala, or Fuji), peeled, cored, and cut in half

2 pears (Bosc), peeled, cored, and cut in half

½ lemon, seeds removed

½ cup toasted and coarsely chopped pecans

1 9-in. whole-wheat pie crust

DESSERTS

skin
smoothing

FOODTRIENTS

Carotenoids
Lauric acid
Potassium
Vitamin C

Sweet Potato and Jackfruit Delight

This dessert is very popular in Asia. Jackfruit, one of the world's largest tree fruits, is very high in antioxidants and has a mild tropical taste. Coconut milk helps hydrate the skin and keep it elastic. Sweet potatoes are packed with carotenoids and potassium.

1. Place the tapioca in cold water in a medium saucepan and slowly bring to a boil. Cook over medium-high heat until tapioca is translucent and soft, about 1–3 minutes. Remove from heat and set aside.

2. Cut the jackfruit into strips and set aside.

3. In a medium saucepan, bring the coconut milk to a boil. Add the sweet potatoes and boil until tender, about 5–10 minutes.

4. Add the jackfruit, sugar, and tapioca to the sweet potato mixture and cook an additional 5 minutes.

5. Serve warm or chilled.

Serves 6–8

¼ cup tapioca

2 cups cold water

1 can (8 oz.) jackfruit, drained of syrup

4 cups coconut milk

1 lb. peeled and cubed yellow and orange sweet potatoes

¼ cup sugar

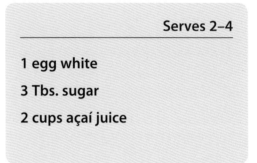

FOODTRIENTS

Anthocyanins
Catechins

Açaí Sorbet

Açaí berries are deep-purple powerhouses, super-rich in antioxidants and anthocyanins. Both properties are great for keeping your body young and healthy. This beautiful frozen confection is very easy to make.

Serves 2–4
1 egg white
3 Tbs. sugar
2 cups açaí juice

1. Using a stand or hand-held mixer, whip the egg white and sugar until soft peaks form, about 5 minutes.

2. Fold in the açaí juice.

3. Transfer the mixture to an ice cream machine. Freeze according to the manufacturer's instructions until the sorbet achieves the texture of soft-serve ice cream, about 30 minutes. You can also freeze overnight inside a plastic container with a tight-fitting lid. To prevent ice crystals from forming, press plastic wrap on the surface of the sorbet and secure the lid tightly on the container.

Drinks

FOODTRIENTS

Anthocyanins
Catechins
Fiber
Omega-3s
Vitamin C

Chia Frescas

Aguas frescas are popular, refreshing fruit drinks found in Mexico. Some roadside vendors add chia seeds to their drinks for extra texture. When soaked, the seeds develop a soft outer coating, somewhat like tapioca. Chia seeds add more than just a textural dimension to fruit drinks; they also provide fiber and the anti-inflammatory Omega-3s. Their nutty flavor goes well with peach tea and strawberry lemonade. They're also nice mixed into sweetened green tea.

1. Soak the chia seeds in the water for 1 hour.

2. To make strawberry lemonade, combine the strawberries, lemon juice, and agave nectar or honey. Mash with a wooden spoon until the fruit is crushed. Add the cold water and stir well.

3. Combine the peach tea and the strawberry lemonade in a pitcher. Add the chia seeds. Top with crushed ice.

Serves 2

2 Tbs. white chia seeds

½ cup water

3 sliced strawberries

2 Tbs. lemon juice (about 1 lemon)

2 Tbs. agave nectar or honey (optional)

1 cup cold water

1 cup chilled peach tea

¼ cup crushed ice

DRINKS

good
digestion

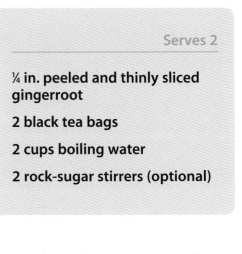

FOODTRIENTS

Catechins
Gingerol

Gingerroot Black Tea

Fresh gingerroot provides protection from inflammation to ease arthritis and allergy symptoms. Black tea has many healthful properties, including flavonoids, which help strengthen blood vessel walls and improve concentration.

Serves 2

¼ in. peeled and thinly sliced gingerroot

2 black tea bags

2 cups boiling water

2 rock-sugar stirrers (optional)

1. Combine the gingerroot and the tea bags in a pitcher with the boiling water. Steep for 1–3 minutes. Strain.

2. Pour into two teacups. Serve with rock-sugar stirrers, if desired.

skin
renewal

FOODTRIENTS

Catechins

Cinnamon Coffee

This delicious cold-weather drink has a host of health benefits. Both cinnamon and nutmeg decrease inflammation inside the body. Cloves have high levels of antioxidants for skin renewal and regeneration. Molasses and evaporated milk provide calcium for strong bones and teeth. And coffee contains antioxidants that help prevent damage to your DNA.

Serves 4

---

1 can (12 oz.) evaporated milk

4 Tbs. molasses (or to taste)

1 tsp. ground cinnamon

¼ tsp. each ground nutmeg and cloves

4 cups freshly brewed coffee

Cinnamon sticks as garnish

---

1. In a medium saucepan, warm the evaporated milk over low heat for 5–10 minutes.

2. Whisk in the molasses, cinnamon, nutmeg, and cloves until milk is frothy and molasses is dissolved.

3. Pour the coffee into 4 cups, add the warm spiced milk to taste, and garnish with cinnamon sticks.

DRINKS

inflammation fighter

FOODTRIENTS

Vitamin C

Mint Agave Tonic

The inspiration for this drink comes from the Cuban mojito. My nonalcoholic version uses sparkling water. Mint leaves aid digestion. The agave nectar is high in fructose, which means that it does not raise your blood sugar to the same extent as other sweeteners do. For a stronger mint flavor, use more mint leaves.

Serves 2

2 small bunches fresh mint leaves

¼ cup lime juice (about 2 limes)

4–8 tsp. agave nectar

2 ½ cups sparkling water

Crushed ice (optional)

1. Place 5–7 mint leaves in each of 2 tall glasses. Bruise the leaves with a cocktail muddle, the handle of a wooden spoon, or the tines of a whisk to help them release their fragrant oil.

2. Mince or chiffonade the remaining mint leaves and divide them equally between the glasses.

3. Add the lime juice, agave nectar, and water in equal amounts. Stir until the agave is dissolved. Add crushed ice to each glass, if desired.

skin
strengthener

Blueberry Hemp-Milk Smoothies

Hemp is the natural fiber from the stalk of a cannabis plant. Hemp seeds and the hemp milk made from them are beneficial to your skin. The Omega-3 fatty acids in hemp seeds help keep skin hydrated and reduce inflammation. Blueberries have tons of antioxidant power and contain protective anthocyanins.

Serves 2

2 cups hemp milk

2 cups fresh blueberries

1 banana

Crushed ice (optional)

Combine the hemp milk, blueberries, and banana in a blender and mix until smooth, about 1 minute. For a cold drink, add crushed ice before blending.

FOODTRIENTS

Anthocyanins
Catechins
Omega-3s
Potassium

DRINKS

age
defying

FOODTRIENTS

Anthocyanins
Catechins
Potassium

Pomegranate Iced Tea

Combining antioxidant-rich pomegranates with the catechins in black tea gives your body extra free-radical-fighting power to combat aging. If pomegranates are too tart for your taste, you can sweeten this tea with honey or use presweetened pomegranate juice. For a stronger drink, stir a teaspoon of instant iced tea into the pomegranate juice.

Serves 2

2 black tea bags

1 cup hot water

1 cup pomegranate juice

2–4 Tbs. honey (optional)

1 cup ice cubes

Pomegranate seeds and slices as garnish

1. In a pitcher, steep the tea bags in hot water for 3 minutes. Remove bags.

2. Add the pomegranate juice and stir well. If using honey, stir in now.

3. To serve, pour into tall glasses over ice and garnish with fresh pomegranate seeds and slices.

skin
softening

FOODTRIENTS

Curcumin
Quercetin
Vitamin C

Turmeric Orange Juice

An ounce or two of turmeric juice mixed with a glass of freshly squeezed orange juice makes a healthy and refreshing beverage. The turmeric and vitamin C in the orange juice double the antioxidant power of this drink. Turmeric also helps reduce inflammation.

Serves 2

2 recipes Fresh Turmeric Juice (page 106)

2 cups freshly squeezed orange juice

Crushed ice (optional)

Combine the Fresh Turmeric Juice and orange juice and divide equally between 2 glasses. Serve at room temperature or over crushed ice, if desired.

FOODTRIENTS

Fiber
Potassium
Probiotics
Vitamin C

Soursop Lassi

A lassi is a drink from India made with yogurt and a pinch of salt. Mango lassis are quite popular in Indian restaurants. I put a South American spin on this healthful drink by using soursop (also known as guanábana) in place of the mango. Soursop provides antioxidants, vitamin C, and riboflavin. Yogurt has beneficial probiotics that aid digestion.

Serves 2

2 cups plain nonfat yogurt

½ tsp. salt

4 Tbs. honey (optional)

2 cups soursop (guanábana) pulp

Mint leaves (optional)

Combine the yogurt, salt, honey (if using), and soursop in a blender and mix at low speed until smooth, about 1–2 minutes. Top with mint leaves, if desired.

Resources

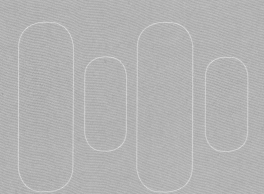

Index

Index

FoodTrients Recipe Benefit index

ANTI-INFLAMMATORY	ANTIOXIDANT	DISEASE-PREVENTING	IMMUNITY BOOSTER	MIND AND BEAUTY		
					STARTERS	
■	■	■		■	Soy Custard Cups	21
■	■	■		■	Quinoa Tabbouleh on Pita	23
■	■	■	■	■	Garlic Crab Royale	25
	■	■	■	■	Moringa Vegetable Soup	27
	■	■	■		Potato Kale Soup	29
■	■	■	■	■	Stuffed Petite Peppers	31
■			■	■	Homemade Sardines	33
	■	■	■	■	Grilled Artichokes with Moringa Dip	34
					SALADS	
■	■	■	■	■	Apple Barley Salad	37
■	■	■	■	■	Beet and Potato Salad	39
■	■	■	■	■	Bitter Melon Salad	41
■	■	■	■	■	Spinach and Grapefruit Salad	43
		■		■	Fig Salad	45
■	■	■	■	■	Lentil Salad	47
■	■	■	■	■	Radish Salad	48
					MAIN COURSES	
					Vegetable	
■	■		■	■	Carrot Quiche	51
■	■	■		■	Green Tea Noodles with Edamame	53
■	■	■	■	■	Tofu and Vegetable Stir-Fry	55
■	■	■	■	■	Buckwheat Crepes	57
					Poultry	
■	■	■	■	■	Summertime Grilled Chicken	59
■	■	■	■	■	Mama's Chicken Sauté	61
■	■	■	■	■	Stuffed Turkey Rolls	63
■	■	■	■	■	Turkey in Turmeric Sauce	65
■	■	■	■	■	Cornish Game Hen and Brown Rice Stew	67
■	■	■	■	■	Whole-Wheat Pasta with Chicken Livers	69

MAIN COURSES

Meat

Anti-Inflammatory	Antioxidant	Disease-Preventing	Immunity Booster	Mind and Beauty		Page
□	■	□	■	□	Meatloaf with Flaxseed	71
□	■	□		□	Pork Loin Pockets	73
□	■	□	■	□	Veal Meatballs with Parsley and Mushroom Gravy	75
□	■	□	■		Spiced Rack of Lamb	77
□	■	□	■	□	Mustard-Crusted Tri-Tip	79

Seafood

Anti-Inflammatory	Antioxidant	Disease-Preventing	Immunity Booster	Mind and Beauty		Page
□	■	□	■	□	Seafood with Wild Rice	81
□	■	□	■	□	Tilapia Fillets with Cilantro	83
□	■	□	■	□	Baked Lobster Tails	85
□	■	□	■	□	Grilled Swordfish in Secret Marinade	87
□	■	□	■	□	Home-Smoked Fish	89
□	■	□	■	□	Homemade Sardines with Tomatoes	91
□	■	□	■	□	Shrimp and Moringa Curry	93
□	■	□	■	□	Whitefish with Turmeric	95
□	■	□	■	□	Shrimp in Tomato Sauce	96

EXTRAS

Anti-Inflammatory	Antioxidant	Disease-Preventing	Immunity Booster	Mind and Beauty		Page
□	■	□	■	□	Honey-Lime Dressing	98
□	■	□		□	Tangy Ginger Dressing	99
□	■	□	■	□	Papaya Salsa	100
□	■	□	■	□	Cranberry Compote	101
□	■	□		□	Savory Stuffing	102
□	■	□			Turmeric Rice	103
□	■	□	■	□	Strawberry-Avocado Relish	104
□	■	□	■	□	Whole-Wheat Garlic Noodles	105
□	■	□			Fresh Turmeric Juice	106

FoodTrients Recipe Benefit index

ANTI-INFLAMMATORY	ANTIOXIDANT	DISEASE-PREVENTING	IMMUNITY BOOSTER	MIND AND BEAUTY		
					DESSERTS	
▪	■	▪	■	▪	Cranberry Bread Pudding	109
▪	■	▪	■	▪	Prune and Walnut Bars	111
▪	■	▪	■	▪	Almond-Blueberry Gelatin Parfaits	113
▪	■	▪	■	▪	Brazil Nut Tarts	115
▪	■	▪	■	▪	Strawberry Tofu	117
▪	■	▪	■	▪	Chia Seed Treat	119
▪	■	▪	■	▪	Mango Tapioca	121
▪	■	▪	■	▪	Pear and Apple Tart	123
▪	■	▪	■	▪	Sweet Potato and Jackfruit Delight	125
	■	▪		▪	Açaí Sorbet	126
					DRINKS	
▪	■	▪	■	▪	Chia Frescas	129
▪			▪	▪	Gingerroot Black Tea	130
		▪		▪	Cinnamon Coffee	131
▪	■	▪	■	▪	Mint Agave Tonic	132
▪		▪		▪	Blueberry Hemp-Milk Smoothies	133
▪	■	▪	■	▪	Pomegranate Iced Tea	134
▪	■	▪	■	▪	Turmeric Orange Juice	135
▪	■	▪	■	▪	Soursop Lassi	136

Useful Equivalents and Metric Conversions

Cooking Measurements

16 tablespoons	=	1 cup
12 tablespoons	=	¾ cup
10 tablespoons + 2 teaspoons	=	⅔ cup
8 tablespoons	=	½ cup
6 tablespoons	=	⅜ cup
5 tablespoons + 1 teaspoon	=	⅓ cup
4 tablespoons	=	¼ cup
2 tablespoons	=	⅛ cup
2 tablespoons + 2 teaspoons	=	⅙ cup
1 tablespoon	=	¹⁄₁₆ cup
2 cups	=	1 pint
2 pints	=	1 quart
3 teaspoons	=	1 tablespoon
48 teaspoons	=	1 cup

Oven Temperatures

250° F	= 120° C
275° F	= 135° C
300° F	= 150° C
325° F	= 160° C
350° F	= 180° C
375° F	= 190° C
400° F	= 200° C
425° F	= 220° C
450° F	= 230° C
475° F	= 245° C
500° F	= 260° C

Conversion Table for Cooking

⅛ teaspoon	=	0.5 milliliter
⅕ teaspoon	=	1 milliliter
¼ teaspoon	=	1.25 milliliters
½ teaspoon	=	2.5 milliliters
¾ teaspoon	=	3.7 milliliters
1 teaspoon	=	5 milliliters
1 ¼ teaspoons	=	6.16 milliliters
1 ½ teaspoons	=	7.5 milliliters
1 ¾ teaspoons	=	8.63 milliliters
2 teaspoons	=	10 milliliters
1 tablespoon (¹⁄₁₆ cup)	=	15 milliliters
2 tablespoons (⅛ cup)	=	29.5 milliliters
⅕ cup	=	47 milliliters
¼ cup (4 tablespoons)	=	59 milliliters
½ cup	=	118.3 milliliters
1 cup	=	237 milliliters
2 cups or 1 pint	=	473 milliliters
3 cups	=	710 milliliters
4 cups or 1 quart	=	.95 liters
4 quarts or 1 gallon	=	3.8 liters
1 fluid oz.	=	30 milliliters (28 grams)
1 pound	=	454 grams

Guide to Age-Defying FoodTrients™

FoodTrient	Potential Benefits
Allicin	Reduces risk of heart disease, heart attack, stroke, cancer.
Anthocyanins	Reduces risk of cancer.
Carotenoids	Reduces risk of heart disease and certain cancers. Supports immune function.
Catechins	Reduces risk of heart disease and heart attack. Protects against certain cancers. Helps prevent dental cavities. May enhance weight loss.
Chlorophyll	Protects against certain cancers.
Choline	Supports healthy brain function and memory. Protects liver. Prevents cholesterol accumulation.
Curcumin	Reduces risk of heart disease, inflammatory conditions, and certain cancers.
Fiber	Reduces risk of heart disease and certain cancers. Aids with appetite control and weight management. Helps prevent constipation. Helps stabilize blood sugar.

Primary Sources	Properties*	Ai	Ao	DP	IB	MB
Fresh garlic	Anti-inflammatory Disease-Preventing	Ai		DP		
Blue, purple, or red fruits and vegetables (esp. berries, grapes, and eggplants)	Disease-Preventing			DP		
Orange vegetables (esp. carrots, pumpkin, sweet potato, winter squash)	Antioxidant Disease-Preventing Immunity Booster		Ao	DP	IB	
Berries, chocolate, grapes, tea	Disease-Preventing Mind and Beauty			DP		MB
Parsley, spinach, watercress, wheatgrass	Antioxidant Disease-Preventing		Ao	DP		
Egg yolks, liver, wheat germ	Disease-Preventing Mind and Beauty			DP		MB
Curry powder, turmeric	Anti-inflammatory Antioxidant Disease-Preventing	Ai	Ao	DP		
Fruits, legumes, vegetables, whole grains	Disease-Preventing Mind and Beauty			DP		MB

Guide to Age-Defying FoodTrients™

FoodTrient	Potential Benefits
Gingerol	Alleviates nausea and inflammatory conditions. Reduces risk of certain cancers.
Indoles	Reduces risk of certain cancers.
Isoflavones	Increases bone density. Reduces risk of cancer and heart disease.
Isothiocyanates	Reduces risk of certain cancers.
Lauric acid	Improves cholesterol balance, prostate health.
Lutein	Reduces risk of age-related macular degeneration and cataracts.
Lycopene	Reduces risk of certain cancers, including lung and prostate.
Oleocanthal/oleuropein	Reduces risk of heart disease, inflammatory disorders.

Primary Sources	Properties*	Ai	Ao	DP	IB	MB
Ginger	Anti-inflammatory Disease-Preventing	Ai		DP		
Cruciferous vegetables (esp. broccoli, Brussels sprouts, cabbage)	Disease-Preventing			DP		
Edamame (soybeans), miso, soy milk, soy sauce, tempeh, tofu	Disease-Preventing Mind and Beauty			DP		MB
Cruciferous vegetables (esp. Brussels sprouts, kale, mustard and turnip greens), horseradish, wasabe	Anti-inflammatory Disease-Preventing	Ai		DP		
Coconut milk, coconut oil	Anti-inflammatory Disease-Preventing	Ai		DP		
Leafy greens (e.g., kale, spinach, collards, and turnip greens)	Antioxidant Disease-Preventing		Ao	DP		
Guava, pink and red grapefruit, tomato products, watermelon	Antioxidant Disease-Preventing		Ao	DP		
Olive oil	Anti-inflammatory Antioxidant Disease-Preventing Mind and Beauty	Ai	Ao	DP		MB

149

Guide to Age-Defying FoodTrients™

FoodTrient	Potential Benefits
Omega-3 fatty acids	Reduces risk of heart disease. Protects against sun damage and skin aging. Protects against dementia.
Potassium	Reduces risk of stroke, osteoporosis, and kidney stones.
Probiotics	Increases resistance to colds and flu. Protects against food-borne illness and inflammatory disorders. Helps prevent constipation.
Quercetin	Reduces inflammation. May reduce allergic sensitivity.
Resveratrol	Reduces risk of heart disease and cancer.
Selenium	Reduces risk of cancer. Increases resistance to infection.
Sulfur compounds	Reduces risk of heart disease and cancer. Supports joints and connective tissue.
Vitamin C	Increases resistance to infection. Reduces risk of cancer, stroke, and cataracts. Protects against sun damage and skin aging.

Primary Sources	Properties*	Ai	Ao	DP	IB	MB
Fish, flaxseed, walnuts	Anti-inflammatory Disease-Preventing Mind and Beauty	Ai		DP		MB
Acorn squash, bananas, lima beans, potatoes, prunes, spinach	Disease-Preventing			DP		
Kefir, unpasteurized sauerkraut, yogurt	Anti-inflammatory Immunity Booster Mind and Beauty	Ai			IB	MB
Onions, apples, broccoli, citrus, kale, onions	Anti-inflammatory	Ai				
Cranberries, grapes, grape juice, peanuts, red wine, red wine vinegar	Anti-inflammatory Disease-Preventing	Ai		DP		
Brazil nuts, mushrooms, poultry, seafood	Antioxidant Disease-Preventing Immunity Booster		Ao	DP	IB	
Garlic, leeks, onions	Anti-inflammatory Disease-Preventing Mind and Beauty	Ai		DP		MB
Berries, citrus, dark green veggies, melons, red peppers	Anti-inflammatory Antioxidant Immunity Booster Mind and Beauty	Ai	Ao		IB	MB

151

Guide to Age-Defying FoodTrients™

FoodTrient	Potential Benefits
Vitamin E	Reduces risk of heart disease. Increases resistance to infection. Protects against sun damage and skin aging. Supports healthy brain function.
Zinc	Increases resistance to infection. Reduces risk of macular degeneration.

*Properties:

 Anti-inflammatory: Reduces inflammation process in cells, tissues, and blood vessels, helping to slow aging and reduce the risk of long-term disease.

 Antioxidant: Prevents and repairs oxidative damage to cells caused by free radicals.

 Disease-Preventing: Reduces risk factors for common degenerative and age-related diseases.

 Immunity Booster: Supports the body's resistance to infection and strengthen immune vigilance and response.

 Mind and Beauty: Encourages vibrant skin and hair and improve mood and mental agility.

Sources: USDA Agricultural Research Service Nutrient Data Laboratory; Linus Pauling Micronutrient Information Center (Oregon State University); U.S. Department of Health and Human Services

Primary Sources	Properties*	Ai Ao DP IB MB
Nuts, vegetable oils, whole grains	Anti-inflammatory Antioxidant Disease-Preventing Mind and Beauty	Ai Ao DP MB
Beef, legumes, nuts, shellfish	Disease-Preventing Immunity Booster	DP IB

Photograph by Gary Moss

Grace O has been baking and cooking professionally and recreationally all of her adult life. As a child in Southeast Asia, she learned the culinary arts by her mother's side in the family cooking school. She became so well versed in hospitality and the culinary arts that she eventually took over the cooking school and opened three restaurants. She is widely credited with popularizing shrimp on sugar-cane skewers and as one of the first culinarians to make tapas a global trend. She has cooked for ruling families and royalty.

Grace O's move to America precipitated a career in healthcare, inspired by her father, who was a physician. Today, she operates skilled nursing facilities in California.

Reigniting her passion for the culinary arts, Grace O strives to create flavorful food using the finest ingredients that ultimately leads to good health. Her recipes, although low in saturated fat, salt, and sugar, are high in flavor. Grace employs spices from all over the world to enliven her dishes, creating food that is different and delicious. She believes that food can be just as effective at fighting aging as the most expensive skin creams. And since she's over 50 herself, she's living proof of that theory.

With more than thirty-five years of experience running restaurants, operating senior healthcare facilities, and studying the healing properties of foods, Grace has established an empowering program of FoodTrients with this cookbook, a Web site (www.FoodTrients.com), and the support of an exemplary board of advisors comprising renowned medical, research, nutrition, and anti-aging experts.